A MANUAL OF BABYLONIAN JEWISH ARAMAIC

David Marcus
Jewish Theological Seminary

D1614275

UNIVERSITY
PRESS OF
AMERICA

LANHAM • NEW YORK • LONDON

Copyright © 1981 by

University Press of America,™ Inc.

4720 Boston Way
Lanham, MD 20706

3 Henrietta Street
London WC2E 8LU England

Library of Congress Cataloging in Publication Data

Marcus, David, 1941-
    A manual of Babylonian Jewish Aramaic.

    "The manual is based on the five following texts:
Baba bathra 58a-58b, Shabbat 156b, Sanhedrin 108b-109b,
Baba mezia 83a-84a, and Berachot 2a-2b."
    Bibliography: p.
    Includes index.
    1. Aramaic language—Grammar. I. Title.
PJ5302.M3   492'.29   80-6073
ISBN 0-8191-1363-8 (pbk.)   AACR2

To the Memory
of my father
J. Y. Marcus

זִכְרוֹ לִבְרָכָה

TABLE OF CONTENTS

PREFACE

This Manual is designed to introduce students to a knowledge of
Babylonian Jewish Aramaic, which is the principle language of the
Babylonian Talmud. The method adopted is the inductive one whereby
grammar is learnt directly as it is encountered in the text. The
texts, on which the Manual is based, are mainly non-legal (aggadic)
thus enabling the student to concentrate more fully on their lin-
guistic aspects. Legal (halachic) texts are, of course, not ignor-
ed, but are left to the later chapters when the student is more
able, from a grammatical point of view, to deal with them. To work
with this Manual the student is expected to have some knowledge of
Hebrew, but not of any other Aramaic dialect. The Manual is hence
geared primarily for beginners in Talmud and Jewish studies, but it
is hoped that more advanced students will profit from it as well.
The author is appreciative of the comments of his students at the
Jewish Theological Seminary during the Manual's period of testing
in the classroom. He is also grateful to the Abbell Publication
Fund of the Jewish Theological Seminary in enabling this book to
be published.

0.1 Babylonian Jewish Aramaic (BJA)

Babylonian Jewish Aramaic is primarily the dialect of the Aramaic parts of the Babylonian Talmud. Together with Mandaic and Syriac it belongs to the Eastern branch of Late Aramaic.

LATE ARAMAIC
(200-900 C.E.)

WEST	EAST
Galilean (Palestinian Talmud, Midrashim, Targumim)	Babylonian Jewish Aramaic Mandaic Syriac
Christian Palestinian	
Samaritan	

The earlier dialects of Aramaic include Official Aramaic (700-300 B.C.E.) of which Biblical Aramaic is a part, and Middle Aramaic (300 B.C.E. - 200 C.E.) of which is included the Aramaic of Targum Onkelos, Targum Jonathan, Qumran texts etc.

0.2 Differences between Eastern and Western Aramaic

Three major differences between Eastern and Western Aramaic are:
(1) The prefix of the 3rd masculine in the imperfect of the verb is with a yod in the West and with a nun or lamed in the East. For example, "he will take" in Western Aramaic is δֿιρֶ֢֜ , in Eastern Aramaic it is either δֿιρֶ֢ or δֿιρֶ֢.
(2) In the East no distinction is made, as is done in the West, between a determined (or definite) noun [e.g. 'the man'] and an

indefinite noun [e.g. 'a man']. For example, מַלְכָּא in Eastern Aramaic means both 'a king' and 'the king', but only 'the king' in Western Aramaic.

(3) The masculine plural of a noun ends in $\bar{e}$ in Eastern Aramaic, but ayyā in Western Aramaic. For example, the plural of 'companion' is חַבְרִין in Eastern Aramaic, but חַבְרַיָּא in Western Aramaic.

0.3 Dialects of BJA

Within BJA there are dialectic differences. Some of the tractates (e.g. Nedarim, Nazir, Meilah, Keritot, Tamid) preserve earlier forms, and these forms occasionally appear in the other tractates including those in our Corpus.

0.4 Corpus of the Manual

The Manual is based on the five following texts: Baba Bathra 58a-58b, Shabbat 156b, Sanhedrin 108b-109b, Baba Mezia 83a-84a, and Berachot 2a-2b. They are referred to throughout in the order of their occurrence by Roman numerals. Thus:

I	Baba Bathra
II	Shabbat
III	Sanhedrin
IV	Baba Mezia
V	Berachot

The Arabic numeral which follows the Roman numeral refers to the line number in the Manual. Thus I:6 means the sixth line of the first text (Baba Bathra), IV:18, the eighteenth line of the fourth text (Baba Mezia) etc.

0.5 Edition used in Manual

The xerocopies of the Talmud text in the Manual are from the standard Vilna edition which, as is well known, is based on Daniel Bomberg's Venice edition of 1520-1531. It was originally printed

2

in 1880-1886, and has since been reprinted and photocopied many times.

0.6 Vocalization of BJA

The Vilna edition of the Talmud is unpointed. The vocalization is aided by vowel letters (matres lectionis) especially aleph, waw, and yod. The aleph may represent a qameṣ (e.g. ʾ אקֿ I:8 = ʾ אָ), occasionally a pataḥ (e.g. אקנ II:15 = אַ), and is written with the diphthong ay (e.g. in ʾ אקֿ I:7). The waw may represent a ḥolem (e.g. אהֿ I:21 = אהֿ), a šureq (e.g. אהואר I:23 = אהֿאר), and occasionally a qameṣ ḥatuph (e.g. ʾקהאר = ʾקהֿאר). The yod may represent both a long and short ḥireq (e.g. long ḥireq אʾ I:9 = אʾ ; short ḥireq אקʾנ I:9 = אקʾנ), ṣere (e.g. אʾאק I:7 = אָאק), and occasionally a seghol (e.g. ʾוהֿ IV:36 = ʾהֿ). Sometimes it is difficult to know when a ḥireq or ṣere is meant (e.g. אʾﬡ I:8, is it אʾﬡ or אʾﬡ ?). Sometimes comparison with other dialects, especially Syriac, will help provide a vocalization.

0.7 Orthography

There are three major features in the orthography of BJA.
(1) When used as consonants, the letters waw and yod are often written twice, e.g. אןʾʾאנ I:5 = אןʾʾאַנ ; אקﬡו IV:78 = אקﬡו .
(2) The laryngeals aleph, hey, chet, & ayin are often interchanged and occasionally dropped. Examples: aleph interchanging with ayin in אﬡ II:8 = אﬡ 'while'; hey interchanging with chet in הֿאקֿ I:20 = חֿאקֿ 'to return'; dropping of a laryngeal in ʾתהﬡ 'under' II:35 = ʾתהﬡ .
(3) Some consonants tend to drop out at the end of a word. Examples:

תﬡ	=	תהﬡ	'again'	I:44
קﬡʾ	=	קﬡʾ ם	'standing'	I:7
אקʾﬡאק	=	אקﬡʾאק	'say!'	I:8
ʾאקʾ	=	אןʾאקʾ	'know'	I:22
אהֿו	=	אןהֿו	'to them'	I:21

3

0.8 Phonetics

BJA follows the rules of Hebrew phonetics. This applies to rules
of vowels in open and closed syllables, to rules of the dagesh,
to rules of the shewa and composite shewa, to rules of laryngeals
affecting the vocalization of preceding and following letters etc.
Examples: In the form הָוָה I:5, the initial hey, being a laryngeal,
has a composite shewa instead of a shewa, and because the final
hey is also a laryngeal the vowel under the waw is a qameṣ not a
pataḥ. This is because, as in Hebrew, the final laryngeal has the
effect of opening a previously closed syllable so that the original
pataḥ of the closed syllable is lengthened to qameṣ. In the form
יָצִיעַ I:9, the ayin has a furtive pataḥ, as is the norm in Hebrew
when an ayin follows a fully accented vowel at the end of a word.

Chapter 1

BABA BATHRA 58a
lines 4-5

ר' בנאה   4
הוה קא מציין מערתא   5

1.1 Translation

"Rabbi Ban'ah used to mark out caves."

1.2 Abbreviations

Abbreviations are marked in the Talmud text by stress marks, ['] for one word, and ["] for two words. Thus over the letter ר in I:4 there is a stress mark 'ר indicating that the letter stands for one word 'רַבִּ 'Rabbi'. In אֲ"ל I:7, there are two stress marks indicating an abbreviation of the words אֲמַר לֵיהּ "he said to him."

1.3 Triliteral root system

One of the major characteristics of Aramaic, and of the Semitic languages in general, is the fact that nearly all verbs can be traced to an original triliteral root. That is, every verb has three root letters which, in the case of strong verbs, will appear in all parts of the verb. Identification of these root letters is essential in analyzing an Aramaic verbal form.

5

1.4 Types of verb

There are two types of verbs, those considered strong and those
considered weak. Strong verbs are those whose root letters have
three strong consonants which will remain in all parts of the
verb. The following consonants are considered strong:

$$N \; \delta \; \ni \; \mathcal{l} \; \mathcal{J} \; \ni \; \mathcal{z} \; \mathcal{A}$$
$$\mathcal{J} \; \mathfrak{e} \; \mathfrak{l} \; \mathfrak{l} \; \mathcal{J} \; \mathcal{J} \; \mathcal{O}$$

Weak verbs are those one or more of whose root letters has a weak
consonant which often drops out in many parts of the verb. The
consonants $\mathcal{J} \; \mathcal{Y} \; \mathfrak{l} \; \mathfrak{n} \; \mathfrak{l} \; \mathfrak{J} \; \mathcal{K}$
are considered weak.

1.5 Verbal nomenclature

As is traditional in Hebrew and Aramaic grammar, the letters $\ni$
(pe̱), $\mathcal{Y}$ (ayin), and δ (lamed), coming from the verb $\delta \mathcal{Y} \ni$,
are used to denote the initial, middle, and final letters of weak
verbs. That is, the first letter of a weak verb is called its
pe̱ letter, the second letter its ayin letter, the third its lamed
letter. Thus, in the verb פַֿ֫ל the first letter starts with a nun,
hence it is termed a Pe Nun verb; in the verb קוּם the middle letter
is waw, so it is termed an Ayin Waw verb; in the verb 'פֶֿ the
last letter is yod, so it is termed a Lamed Yod verb.

1.6 Conjugations

There are six conjugations in BJA: three active and three reflexive.
The active conjugations are: Qal, Pael, & Aphel, which correspond
respectively to the Hebrew Qal, Piel, & Hiphil conjugations. The
reflexive conjugations are: Ithpeal, Ithpaal, & Ittaphal, which all
correspond to the Hebrew Hithpael conjugation. The Ittaphal is
very rare, and indeed does not occur in our Corpus. The two verbs
that appear in this chapter are הֲוָה and אֲזִ֫ן I:5: the verb
הֲוָה is in the Qal conjugation, while אֲזִ֫ן is in the Pael.
The Pael, like the Hebrew Piel, serves as a factitive (< Latin

6

factitare 'to do often', 'to practice', 'to declare [someone] to
be'), and is characterized by a dagesh in the second root letter.

1.7 Tenses

There are three tense forms in BJA: perfect, imperfect, and participle. The perfect corresponds to our past tense, the imperfect
to our future, while the participle may correspond to our past,
present, or future depending on the context. With regard to the
two verbal forms in this chapter, the first one נֲוָה is a perfect
tense form, while the second אֹצ֖ין is a participle form.

1.8 Qal 3rd masculine singular perfect

The 3rd masculine singular perfect Qal of a strong verb is קְטַל ,
cf. נְבַק I:9. The form הֲוָה is the 3rd masculine singular
perfect of the weak verb הוי . As has already been noted (#0.8),
it takes a composite shewa instead of a shewa because of the
initial hey, and it has a qames instead of a patah because of the
final hey.

1.9 Qal active participle

The paradigm forms of the active participle of a strong verb in
the Qal conjugation are:

קָטֵל	masculine singular
קָטְלָה \ קָטֶלֶת	feminine singular
קָטְלִי	masculine plural
קָטְלָן	feminine plural

The first occurrence of these forms in the Corpus are:

	I:7	צָאֵיב	masculine singular
IV:91	I:25	צַאנְיָה	feminine singular
	I:22	בָּאֵי	masculine plural
	IV:87	סָקְלָן	feminine plural

7

1.10 Pael active participle

The paradigm forms of the active participle in the <u>Pael</u> conjugation are:

מְקַבֵּל	masculine singular
מְקַבְּלָא	feminine singular
מְקַבְּלִי	masculine plural
מְקַבְּלָן	feminine plural

The first occurrences of these forms in the Corpus are:

I:28	מְבַאֵל	I:5	מְאַגֵּן	masculine singular
		I:8	מְצַעֲרָא	feminine singular
		III:89	מְסַדְּרִין	masculine plural
			—	feminine plural

1.11 Use of the form קָא

The form קָא (originally a participle from the verb קָאֵם : קוּם > קָאֵי > קָא) serves to introduce a participle form. It may stand alone as here קָא מְאַגֵּן , or it may be joined to the participle form, e.g. קָאָמַר I:22. It is important to note that the form following קָא must be a participle.

1.12 Perfect of הֲוֵי with the active participle

The perfect of הֲוֵי with the active participle may denote (a) the simple past tense as, for example, לָא הֲוו יָדְעֵי "they did not know" I:22, or (b) the frequentative past 'he used to do something', as, for example, here in I:4-5 רַבָּי בַּנְאָה הֲוָה קָא מְאַגֵּן מְעָרָתָא "Rabbi Ban'ah used to mark out caves," or in הֲוָה קָטֵל שִׁכְבֵי "he used to exhume corpses" I:18.

1.13 The noun

As previously noted (#0.2) one of the characteristics of BJA is the fact that there is no distinction between definiteness and indefiniteness in a noun. Thus, בָּבָא I:7 can mean 'a gate' or 'the

8

gate'. The paradigm of the noun ܛܒܐ 'a good one' is:

	PLURAL		SINGULAR	
	ܛܒ̈ܐ		ܛܒܐ	MASCULINE
	ܛܒ̈ܬܐ		ܛܒܬܐ	FEMININE

The first occurrences of these forms in the Corpus are:

	PLURAL			SINGULAR	
I:18	ܒܛܐ̈		I:7	ܛܒܐ	MASCULINE
I:5	ܐܪ̈ܝܟܬܐ		I:5	ܐܪܝܟܬܐ	FEMININE

Chapter 2

BABA BATHRA 58a
lines 5-9

כי מטא למערתא 5
דאברהם אשכחה לאליעזר עבד אברהם 6
דקאי קמי בבא א"ל מאי קא עביד אברהם 7
א"ל גאני בכנפה דשרה וקא מעיינא ליה ברישה א"ל זיל אימא ליה בנאה 8
קאי אבבא 9

2.1 Translation

When he arrived at the cave of Abraham he found Eliezer, Abraham's
servant, standing in front of the gate. "What is Abraham doing?"
said he. "He is lying in Sarah's lap, and she is watching over
him." "Go and tell him that Ban'ah is at the gate!"

2.2 Lamed Aleph verbs

One of the features that BJA has in common with Mishnaic Hebrew
is the fact that <u>Lamed Aleph</u> verbs are treated like <u>Lamed Yod</u> verbs.
However, in the 3rd person masculine singular perfect of both <u>Lamed</u>
<u>Aleph</u> and <u>Lamed Yod</u> verbs, an <u>aleph</u> often occurs. Examples:
<u>Lamed Aleph</u>: מְטָא 'he arrived' I:5; אֲתָא 'he came' I:19
<u>Lamed Yod</u>: חֲזָא 'he saw' I:35; בְּעָא 'he requested' III:3.

2.3 Expression of the construct

There are three ways of expressing the construct case: (1) by use
of the genitive indicator דְּ , as in מְעָרְתָּא דְּאַבְרָהָם 'the cave of
Abraham' = 'Abraham's cave' I:5-6; (2) by use of a proleptic

11

suffix and the genitive indicator בְּ , e.g. בַּנְפַּהּ דְּשָׂרָה 'her lap of
Sarah' = 'Sarah's lap' I:8; (3) by use of a special construct form.
This construction is more a feature of earlier Aramaic, but it
does occur in BJA with some common nouns, e.g. בֵּי מַלְכָּא 'court
of the king' = 'the king's court' I:29; בַּר יִשְׂרָאֵל 'son of Israel'
= 'an Israelite', 'a Jew' II:7.

Possible Ways of Expressing 'The Man's Son'

(1) Genitive indicator   בְּרָא   דְּגַבְרָא

(2) Genitive indicator +
     proleptic suffix   בְּרֵיהּ   דְּגַבְרָא

(3) Special construct   בַּר   גַּבְרָא

2.4 Aphel conjugation

The paradigm form of the 3rd masculine singular perfect of a strong
verb in the Aphel conjugation is אַקְטֵל . The Aphel conjugation corresponds to the Hebrew Hiphil, and has primarily the force of a
causative "causing something to be done", e.g. קְטַל 'he killed',
אַקְטֵל 'he caused to kill'; אֲתָא 'he came' I:19; אַיְתֵי "he
caused (scissors) to come" = "he brought (scissors)" I:20. Sometimes there is no special nuance of a verb being in the Aphel conjugation, e.g. אַשְׁכַּח 'he found' II:9. In אַשְׁכְּחֵיהּ I:6, the 3rd
masculine singular form אַשְׁכַּח has a pronominal suffix ◌ֵיהּ 'him',
thus, it literally means 'he found him'.

2.5 Suffixes

The suffixes to the verb, noun, and preposition are essentially
the same. A paradigm of the suffixes may be obtained by using the
prepositions מִן 'from' and לְ 'to' since most of their forms
occur in the Corpus.

SINGULAR

I:26	אָֽנ	IV:98	אָנָ'אִ	1st common
III:15	ךְָ	I:19	אָנָךְ	2nd masculine
	ךְָ		אָנָךְ	2nd feminine
I:8	הּ'ָ	I:38	אָנָ'הּ	3rd masculine
II:21	הָּ	IV:44	אָנָ'הָּ	3rd feminine

PLURAL

IV:3	נָ	II:5	אָנָ	1st common
I:23	וֹכָ	I:28	אָנָ"כוֹ	2nd masculine
	כָ		אָנָ"כֵ'	2nd feminine
I:21	וֹהָ	I:27	אָנָ"הוֹ	3rd masculine
	'הָ		אָנָ"הֵ'	3rd feminine

The first occurrences of nouns with suffixes in the Corpus are:

SINGULAR

		1:21	אַרָא'	1st common
II:34	רֵעֵ'ךְ:	IV:97	חֵלָךְ	2nd masculine
		II:33	אַרְךְ	2nd feminine
		I:8	רֵעֵ'הּ	3rd masculine
		I:8	בֵּנָפֵסּ	3rd feminine

PLURAL

V:49	אַתְנָתָ'ן	IV:32	רַבָּנָ	1st common
		IV:3	אַגָרָ"כוֹ	2nd masculine
		T:49	פָּרָ"הוֹ	3rd masculine

2.6 Proleptic suffixes

A common stylistic feature of BJA is the use of proleptic or anti-
cipatory suffixes. In the phrase אַשְׁכְּחֵהּ the suffix הּ'ָ 'him' on
אַשְׁכַּח anticipates the following object 'Eliezer', so it literally
means "he found him, Eliezer." The suffix is in effect redundant,
as the same meaning is yielded with אַשְׁכַּח'אֱלִיעֶזֶר .

13

2.7 Preposition ל as indicator of direct object

When used as a preposition, ל means 'to', 'for', 'unto' etc.
However, it may also be used as an indicator of the direct object,
as, for example, in לֵיהּ אֲזִינָא קָא "she is watching him" I:8.
Occasionally it is preceded by a proleptic suffix, as in אַשְׁכְּחַהּ
לֶאֱלִיעֶזֶר "he found Eliezer" I:6.

2.8 Redundant use of the relative pronoun

Another stylistic feature of BJA is a redundant use of the relative
pronoun דְ, that is, a use of the relative pronoun which is not
necessary for the syntax. Thus, the following phrases could stand
syntactically without the relative pronoun:

אַשְׁכְּחַהּ לֶאֱלִיעֶזֶר עֶבֶד אַבְרָהָם דְקָאֵי אַתַּרְעָא
"he found Eliezer, Abraham's servant, standing before the gate"
I:6-7; חֲדָא אֶלָּא נְקַטִי בְּקֶרֶן "I have only taken one" III:62.

2.9 Qal active participle of Ayin Waw and Ayin Yod verbs

The active participle (#1.9) of middle weak verbs in the Qal conjugation may be observed from the verbs קוּם 'to stand' and מִית
'to die'.

II:7	מָאֵית	I:7	קָאֵי	masculine singular
II:21	מָיְתָא		קָיְמָא	feminine singular
	מָיְתֵי	III:82	קָיְמֵי	masculine plural
	מָיְתָן		קָיְמָן	feminine plural

It will be noted that whereas yods appear in the feminine singular
and both plurals, in the masculine singular either an aleph or a
yod may appear depending on the type of verb. For the dropping
of the mem in the form קָאֵי , see #0.7, but note its retention
with the enclitic pronoun קָאֵימְנָא , #3.9.

14

2.10 Qal active participle of Lamed Yod verbs

The active participle Qal of Lamed Yod verbs may be seen from the following forms which appear in the Corpus:

I:8	אָזֵ֠ל	masculine singular
IV:103	בָּכְיָא	feminine singular
I:32	אָזֵ֠ל	masculine plural
	[בָּכְיָן]	feminine plural

2.11 Imperative of Pe Aleph verbs

The imperative mood indicates a command. The paradigm masculine singular form of the strong verb in the Qal conjugation is פְּעֹל cf., פְּעַ֠ל III:14. The imperative forms of the verb אֲזַל 'to go' are:

I:8	זִיל	masculine singular
	זִילִי	feminine singular
I:27	זִילוּ	common plural

Other imperative forms of Pe Aleph verbs which appear in the Corpus are: אֵימָא (from אֲמַר 'to speak') I:8 and תָא (from אֲתָא 'to come') IV:28.

2.12 The preposition אַ

The preposition אַ is attached to a word together with a dagesh, and stands for the prepositions לְ 'to', 'unto', or עַל 'over', 'by', 'against'. For example, בָּנְאָה קְאֵי אַבָּבָא "Ban'ah is at the gate" I:8-9.

15

Chapter 3

BABA BATHRA 58a
lines 9-17

9 א"ל ליעול מידע ידיע דיצר בהאי עלמא ליכא עייל ונפק כי
10 מטא למערתא דאדם הראשון יצתה בת קול ואמרה נסתכלת בדמות דיוקני
11 בדיוקני עצמה אל תסתכל הא בעינא לציוני מערתא כמדת החיצונה כך
12 מדת הפנימית ולמ"ד *שני בתים זו למעלה מזו כמדת עליונה כך מדת
13 התחתונה א"ר בנאה נסתכלתי בשני עקביו ודומים לשני גלגלי חמה הבל
14 בפני שרה כקוף בפני אדם שרה בפני חוה כקוף בפני אדם חוה בפני
15 אדם כקוף בפני אדם אדם בפני שבינה כקוף בפני אדם *ישופריה דרב כהנא
16 (מעין שופריה דרב שופריה דרב) מעין שופריה דרבי אבהו שופריה דר' אבהו
17 מעין שופריה דיעקב אבינו שופריה דיעקב אבינו מעין שופריה דאדם הראשון

3.1 Qal imperfect of Double Ayin verbs

The paradigm forms of the 3rd masculine singular imperfect of the
strong verb in the Qal conjugation are $\delta_I \zeta \hbar \delta$ and $\delta_I \zeta \hbar \jmath$, cf.,
$\delta_I \hbar \check{\zeta} \delta$ III:58 and $\delta_I \hbar \check{\zeta} \jmath$ III:53. Forms of the imperfect of a
Double Ayin verb like $\delta \delta \aleph$ 'to enter' are $\delta_I \aleph \check{\delta}$ I:9 or $\delta_I \aleph \jmath$.
Note that the imperfect may have a future meaning, e.g. "he will
enter," or it may express a wish, e.g. "let him enter."

3.2 Qal infinitive

The infinitive form of a strong verb in the Qal conjugation is
$\delta \zeta \hbar \aleph$, cf., אֶכְתַּב I:46. Other infinitives of the Qal which
occur in the Corpus are: אֱ'צֶ I:9 of the Pe Yod verb 'צֶ
'to know'; אֱ'מַ,ת I:45 of the Ayin Waw verb תוֹ,ם 'to die';
אֱ'בָ,ת III:3 of the Ayin Yod verb ב'ת 'to lodge'; אֱמֵ'צ IV:76
of the Lamed Yod verb ח'צ 'to see'.

17

3.3 Qal passive participle

The paradigm forms of the passive participle of a strong verb in
the Qal conjugation are:

הָקֻ׳לֹּ	masculine singular
הָקֻ׳לֹאָ	feminine singular
הָקֻ׳לִֹ׳	masculine plural
הָקֻ׳לֹֹ	feminine plural

The first occurrences of these forms in the Corpus are:

I:9	יָ׳דֻ֑עַ	masculine singular
IV:1	פְּ׳עֻ׳לָה	feminine singular
II:15	פְּקֻ׳דִֹ׳	masculine plural
–		feminine plural

The passive participle is so called because it signifies "something
is done." Thus, from כָּתַב 'to write', כָּתֻב means 'it is
written'; from יָדַ׳ע 'to know', יָדֻ׳עַ means 'it is known'.

3.4 Infinitive with finite form of verb

The infinitive is often used with a finite form of the verb (one
which distinguishes person, number, tense, or mood) for emphasis.
Examples: יָדֹעַ יֻדַ׳ע "it is well-known" I:9; הָתֵל מְהַתְּלִ׳ם
"they are surely mocking" III:7.

3.5 Demonstrative pronouns

The forms of the demonstrative pronouns are:

	FEMININE				MASCULINE		
'THIS'	זֹאת	I:11	זֹה	‖	זֶה	I:9	זֶה
'THAT'	הַהִיא	I:25	הִיא	‖ I:18	הַהוּא		הַהוּא

	COMMON			
		אֵלֶּה		אֵל
'THESE'				
'THOSE'	IV:79v.	הָהֵ׳נָה	II:5	הָהֵם

18

The demonstrative pronouns normally precede the noun, for example,
ﭏﻦﭏﻼ 'ﻦﭏﻼﭏ 'in this world' I:9.

3.6 The form ﻦﭏﻼ

The form ﻦﭏﻼ I:9 is made up of the form ﻦﭏﻼ 'there is not' I:26,
and the form ﻦﭏﻼﭏ 'there is' I:30 (which itself comes from ﻦﭏﻼ
'there is' + ﻦﭏﻼ 'here'), and means 'there is not (here)'.

3.7 Pael 3rd masculine singular perfect

The 3rd masculine singular perfect Pael of the strong verb is
ﭏﭏﭏ , cf., ﭏﭏﭏﭏ IV:32. The forms of the 3rd masculine singular
perfect Pael of weak verbs which appear in the Corpus are:

Ayin Waw	ﭏﭏﭏ	'he examined'	I:9
Double Ayin	ﭏﭏﭏ	'he entered'	I:9
Lamed Yod	ﭏﭏﭏ	'he taught'	IV:11

Note that the forms of the Ayin Waw and the Double Ayin are the
same in the Pael conjugation.

3.8 The demonstrative ﻦﭏﻼ

The feminine demonstrative pronoun ﻦﭏﻼ 'this' may be used adversatively (to express contrariety, opposition, or antithesis).
For example, ﭏﭏﭏﭏ ﻦﭏﻼ "but I seek" I:11.

3.9 Active participle with enclitics

The active participle may be joined with a shortened form of the
personal pronoun, called an enclitic, to make a combined form.
For example, the shortened form of the 1st person singular pronoun
ﭏﭏﭏ 'I' is ﭏﭏ . It is joined to the participle as follows:
ﭏﭏ + ﭏﭏﭏ = ﭏﭏﭏﭏﭏ . Examples in the Corpus of the participle joined to the 1st person enclitic are:

ﭏﭏﭏﭏ	(ﭏﭏ +	ﭏﭏﭏ	) I:11
ﭏﭏﭏﭏﭏ	(ﭏﭏ +	ﭏﭏﭏ	) II:14
ﭏﭏﭏﭏﭏ	(ﭏﭏ +	ﭏﭏﭏ	) II:14

Note the dropping of the final letter in כְּאִנָא , #0.7, but its retention in הָאִנָּא , #2.9. Note also the feminine הָאִנָּא in II:28 instead of the expected הָ ::אִנָא < הָ :: אִנָּא + כָ , #2.9.

3.10 Pael infinitive

The Pael infinitive form is הַקּוֹלָ , cf., אֲפֵיר ' III:b. With the Ayin Yod verb ס' ג it is ג"יל' I:11, and with the Lamed Yod verb גַ ל' it is גַ ל'' II:33.

Chapter 4

BABA BATHRA 58a
lines 18-24

18 ההוא אמגושא דהוה הטיט שכבי כי מטא אמערתא דרב טובי בר מתנה
19 תפשיה (6) בדיקניה אתא אביי א"ל במטותא מינך שבקיה לשנה אחריתי
20 הדר אתא תפשיה בדיקניה אתא אביי לא שבקיה עד דאייתי מספרא
21 וגזיא לדיקניה ההוא דאמר להו הביתא דעפרא להד בראי חביתא דגרמי
22 להד בראי חביתא *דאודרא להד בראי לא הוו ידעי מאי קאמר להו אתו
23 לקמיה דרבי בנאה אמר להו אית לכו ארעא אמרו ליה אין אית לכו חזותא (נ)
24 אין אית לכו בסתרקי אינאי הבי הבי קאמר לכו

4.1 The demonstrative הַ וְ וC·ּ

The masculine demonstrative הַ וְ IC·ּ 'that' may also mean 'a certain one', e.g. in פָּ אְ וַ רֹ הַ ו·IC "a certain (man) said to them" I:21. It may also modify a noun with the same meaning, e.g. IC ו אNIC הַ וְ ו·IC 'a certain magician' I:18.

4.2 Relative pronoun emphasizing a subject

The relative pronoun יְ often occurs after a subject for emphasis. Examples: 'שְ כָּ אִ חָ מְ לֹ וּ בַּ הְ וְ וָ IC ו אNIC הַ ו·IC "a certain magician used to exhume corpses" I:18; יֹ וְ פֿ פָּ אִ וַ רֹ הַ ו·IC "a certain (man) said to them" I:21; יֹ וְ תֵּ גְּ בְ פַ פְּ אְ וַ צָ א אַ בָ רְ ICַ הַ ו·IC "a certain man heard his wife" I:24.

4.3 Qal active participle of Double Ayin verbs

The active participle Qal of Double Ayin verbs may be seen from the following forms which appear in the Corpus:

I:18   חֲ֫עִל   I:18v.   חֲ֫"ל   masculine singular

II:20   צַ֫"כֶה   feminine singular

III:84   אֶ֫"כ֫י   masculine plural

[צַ֫"כֶן]   feminine plural

Note that there are two forms of the masculine singular חֲ֫עִל &
חֲ֫"ל . The form חֲ֫"ל is identical to certain forms of the
active participle <u>Qal</u> of <u>Ayin Waw/Yo</u>d verbs, e.g. אָ֫"ת II:7, #2.9.

4.4 Imperative plus suffixes

The suffixes attached to the masculine singular imperative of a
strong verb are the same as those attached to the perfect (for the
suffixes, see #2.5). Thus, the form עֲזָבֹהּ means both 'he left
him' I:20, and 'leave him!' I:19. Other forms of the masculine
singular imperative plus suffixes which occur in the Corpus are:
תָּפֹסֹהּ 'seize him' IV:35; יַ֫הַבָהּ 'give her' III:67; הַבָהּ 'give
it' III:68.

4.5 Absolute case

Alongside the regular form of the noun (#1.13) is a less frequent
one called the absolute. The forms of the absolute are:

PLURAL	SINGULAR	
כֲבִ֫י	כֲב֫	MASCULINE
כֲבָ֫ן	כֲבָ֫א	FEMININE

The first occurrences of these forms in the Corpus are:

PLURAL		SINGULAR		
I:43	חַ֫"ל ‖	I:21	חֲב	MASCULINE
I:47	כִסֹ֫וּ ‖ III:85	בֹ֫אֹיכ I:19	כֶסֶ֫ה	FEMININE

4.6 Auxiliary use of הַבֶר

The verb הַבֶר (< חַבֶר #0.7) 'to return' is sometimes used as an

22

auxiliary meaning 'again'. For example, ⟨ܐܬ̣ܐ ܬܘܒ ܒܫܢ̱ܬ̇ܐ ܕܒܬ̇ܪܗ⟩ "he came again the following year" I:19-20.

4.7 The form ܐܝ̣ܬܝ

The form ܐܝ̣ܬܝ is a 3rd masculine singular _Aphel_ perfect of the doubly weak verb ܐܬ̣ܐ 'to come'. It is doubly weak because it is both _Pe Aleph_ and _Lamed Aleph_.   It is also outstanding in the fact that whereas _Aphels_ of _Pe Aleph_ verbs are found with a _waw_, e.g. ܐܘܟܠ· from ܐܟܠ 'to eat', the _Aphel_ of ܐܬ̣ܐ occurs both with a _yod_ as here ܐܝ̣ܬܝ 'he brought' I:20, and without a _yod_, as in ܐܝܬܝܘ·ܗܝ 'they brought him' I:31, and ܐܝܬܝܘ·ܗ̇ 'they brought him' IV:37.

4.8 Alternate form of the participle

The masculine singular active participle form is ܩܿܐܡ (#1.9). However, an alternate form ܩܿܐܡܐ or ܩܿܐܡܗ is also found. Thus, alongside ܩܿܐܡ is found ܩܿܐܡܐ I:28; alongside ܐܬܐ is found ܐܬ̣ܝܐ I:21. There is no difference in meaning in this alternate form.

4.9 Meanings of the active participle

Depending on the context the active participle may indicate acts in the past, present, or future. Examples:

PAST

a. Perfect

ܐܝ̣ܬܝ ܡܣܦܪ̈ܐ ܘܓܙ̣ܐ ܕܩܢܗ·ܗ "he brought scissors and cut off his beard" I:20-21

ܗܟ̣ܢ ܐܡ̣ܪ ܠܟܘܢ "thus he said to you" I:24

b. Continuous past

ܡܢ ܐܡ̣ܪ ܠܗܘܢ "what he was saying to them" I:22

ܟܕ ܡ̇ܐܬ "when he was dying" I:26

PRESENT

כֵ אֶשְׁכַּח לֵיעֶזֶר עַבְדָּא דְּאַבְרָהָם קָאֵם בְּקִרְבָא דְּתַרְעָא

"He found Eliezer, Abraham's servant, standing in front of the gate"
I:6-7

מָה עָבֵד קָא אַבְרָהָם "What is Abraham doing?" I:7

FUTURE

אַשְׁקְיוֹהִי חַמְרָא וְיִחְיֵי "they give him wine to drink and he will
live" I:45

אֲזַל וְלָא יָתֵב וְיִכְתְּשֵׁינֵהּ חִוְיָא וִימוּת "he will go and will not
return, a snake will bite him and he will die" II:6-7

4.10 Plural suffixes

The suffixes attached to the plural noun are similar to those
attached to the singular (#2.5). Thus, עַבְדָּי may mean 'my
slave' or 'my slaves', רֵישָׁיִךְ II:34 'your head' or 'your heads'.
Sometimes a different stem will be used to differentiate between
singular and plural, e.g. בְּרִי = 'my son' I:22, but בְּנַי = 'my sons'.

4.11 Apposition

Two nouns standing together in the same number, case, and gender
(and which are not joined together in a construct-genitive relation-
ship, #2.3) are said to be in apposition. Adjectives are the best
example of apposition. The phrase גַּבְרָא טָבָא 'the good man' is
literally 'the man, the good one' where טָבָא is standing in
apposition to גַּבְרָא . Examples: לְחַד בְּרִי , literally "to one,
my son" = 'my one son' I:22; כּוֹלְהוֹן טוּבַיָּא , literally "all of them,
the goods" = 'all the goods' I:29.

4.12 Qal 3rd masculine plural perfect

One of the two forms of the 3rd masculine plural perfect Qal of
a strong verb is קְטַלוּ , cf., אֲמַרוּ I:23. For a Lamed Yod
verb the plural is like הֲווֹ 'they were' I:22 (from הֲוָה), and
אֲתוֹ 'they came' I:22 (from אֲתָא).

24

4.13 Possession

Possession is expressed by the particle of existence אִית and
the preposition לְ (cf., Hebrew יֵשׁ + לְ). Examples:
אִית לָךְ אַרְעָא literally, "there is to you land" = "you have land,"
in context of I:23 "do you have any land?"; אַרְעָה בְּנֵי עֲשָׂר לִי אִית
"I had ten children" I:25-26. The negative is formed by לְ + לִית ,
e.g. לִית לִי , literally, "there were not to me" = "I did not
have" I:26.

Chapter 5

BABA BATHRA 58a
lines 24-34

ההואגברא דשמעה לדביתהו 24
25 דקא אמרה לברתה אמאי לא צניעת באיסורא הך איתתא עשרה בני
26 אית לה ולית לי מאבוך אלא חד כי שכיב אמר לה כל נכסי לחד
27 ברא לא ידעי להו מינייהו אתו לקמיה דרבי בנאה אמר להו זילו חבוטו
28 קברא דאבוכן עד דקאי ומגלי לכו להי מינייכו שבקא אזלו כולהו ההוא
29 דבריה הוה לא אזל אמר להו כולהו נכסי דהאי אזלו אכלו קורצא בי מלכא
30 אמרי איכא גברא חד ביהודאי דקא מפיק ממונא מאנשי בלא סהדי
31 ובלא (ו) מידי אתיוהו חבשוהו אזלא דביתהו אמרה להו עבדא חד הוה לי
32 פסקן לרישיה ופשטו למשכיה ואכלו בישריה וקא מלו ביה מיא ומשקן ביה
33 לחברייא ולא קא יהבי לי דמי ולא אגריה לא ידעי מאי קא אמרה להו אמרי
34 ניתו לחכימא דיהודאי ולימא קריוהו לר' בנאה אמר להו זרנוקא אמרה לכו

5.1 The form בְּ'תְהוּ

The form בְּ'תְהוּ 'his wife' I:24 literally means 'of their
house'. It is made up of the genitive indicator בְּ and בֵּ'תְהוּ
'their house'. Note that the expected form 'his house' would
be בֵּ'תֵ'הּ , #2.5.

5.2 Qal passive participle with enclitics

Like the present participle (#3.9), the passive participle (#3.3)
may be joined with shortened forms of the personal pronouns to
produce the following forms:

PLURAL		SINGULAR		
קְ'לֵ'נַן = נַן + קְ'לֵ'		קְ'לֵ'נָא = אַנָ + קְ'לֵ'		1st PERSON
קְ'לֵ'תוּ = אַתוּ + קְ'לֵ'		קְ'לֵ'תְ = אַתְ + קְ'לֵ'		2nd PERSON

27

The only example of a passive participle plus enclitic in our
Corpus is in the form ﾖﾏﾏﾖﾏ I:25 which is a passive participle
of צﾏﾖ 'to be discreet' plus the 2nd person enclitic, e.g.
ﾖﾏﾏ + צﾏﾖ = ﾖﾏﾏﾖﾏ.

5.3 Expressing the first person impersonally

Sometimes in order to avoid using the first person pronoun a cir-
cumlocution is employed. The phrase 'that man' or 'that woman'
is then used to refer to the speaker. Examples: ﾏﾏﾏ ﾏﾏ
ﾏﾏ ﾏﾏﾏ ﾏﾏ ﾏﾏﾏﾏ , literally, "that woman had ten
children" = "I had ten children" I:25-26;   ﾏﾏ ﾏﾏﾏﾏﾏ
ﾏﾏﾏﾏ ﾏﾏﾏ ﾏﾏﾏﾏ , literally, "they will strip the
garment from that man" = "they will strip my garment" III:89-90.

5.4 Suffixes to ﾏﾏﾏ

With the noun ﾏﾏﾏ 'father', the suffixes (other than the first
person singular) are attached to the stem ﾏﾏﾏ .   Examples which
occur in the Corpus are:

ﾏﾏﾏﾏ	'your father'	I:26
ﾏﾏﾏﾏ	'her father'	II:26
ﾏﾏﾏﾏﾏ	'your (plural) father'	I:28
ﾏﾏﾏﾏﾏ	'their father'	T:45

5.5 Qal plural imperative

The masculine singular imperative of a strong verb is ﾏﾏﾏ ,
#2.11. The feminine is ﾏﾏﾏ , while the plural (common) is
ﾏﾏﾏ . The first occurrences of imperative forms of strong
verbs in the Corpus are:

III:14	ﾏﾏﾏ	MASCULINE SINGULAR
I:27	ﾏﾏﾏ	COMMON PLURAL

Note that the plural imperative of the Pe Aleph verb ﾏﾏﾏ , is
ﾏﾏﾏ , #2.11.

5.6 Retention of nun

In some suffixed or plural forms, a <u>nun</u>, which is normally dropped
at the end of a word (#0.7), is occasionally retained. This retention is characteristic of older Aramaic, but it appears sporadi-
cally in BJA. Examples: אֶלְ הֶ דֹ גֹ I:28 for אֶלְ הֶ דֹ ; פֹ הֹ נ III:85
alongside פֹ הֹ ד I:21; אֲמַ נְ הֹ ' I:38 for אֲמַ הֹ ' .

5.7 Quantitative pronoun

The quantitative pronoun כֹּ לָ א 'all' may stand in the construct
before the word it qualifies, e.g. כֹּ ל מוֹ תָ א 'every death' I:42.
Alternatively, it can stand in apposition (#4.11) with the quali-
fying word. In the latter case it must have the appropriate 3rd
person pronominal suffix, e.g. כֹּ לְ הוֹ ן נִ כְ סַ יָ א , literally, "all of
them, the goods" 'all the goods' I:29. In the phrases כֹּ לְ '(כִּ)
'to such an extent' I:35, and כֹּ לְ ' עֲ נָ שׁ 'everyone' II:27, one
would have expected both forms כֹּ לְ ' to have a 3rd person masculine
singular pronominal suffix, e.g. כֹּ לְ ' הּ .

5.8 Genitive indicator used as predicate

The genitive indicator דְ 'of', 'belonging to' may be used as a
predicate, that is, with verbal force meaning "belongs to." For
example, כֹּ לְ הוֹ ן נִ כְ סַ יָ א דְ הָ אי "all the goods belong to this one"
I:29.

5.9 Aphel active participle

The paradigm forms of the active participle of a strong verb in
the <u>Aphel</u> conjugation are:

אַ קְ טֵ ל	masculine singular
אַ קְ טְ לָ א	feminine singular
אַ קְ טְ לִ '	masculine plural
אַ קְ טְ לָ ן	feminine plural

The first occurrences of these forms with strong verbs in the
Corpus are:

29

| I:37 | אַ צֵ נ' | masculine singular |
| IV:55 | אַ סֹ נ ֹ ח' | masculine plural |

Forms of the <u>Aphel</u> participle of a <u>Pe Nun</u> verb may be observed from the verb נפק 'to go out'.

I:30	אַ פֵ ק'	masculine singular
III:91	נ פֵ קַ א	feminine singular
IV:54 אַ פֵ קִ ן	I:38 אַ פֵ ק' נ'	masculine plural

The masculine plural of an <u>Ayin Waw</u> verb (e.g. קום) may be either אַ קֵ"מִ' III:7 or אַ קֵ"מֵ ו T:44.

The first occurrences of <u>Aphel</u> participles of <u>Lamed Yod</u> verbs in the Corpus are:

| III:51 | נ ֹ גֵ אַ' | masculine singular |
| I:32 אַ סֵ קֵ ו | III:83 אַ גֵ נ' | masculine plural |

5.10 Qal 3rd feminine singular perfect

The 3rd feminine singular perfect <u>Qal</u> of a strong verb is קְ טֵ לַ ת or קְ טַ לַ ת . Examples: אַ זַ לַ ת 'she went' I:31; אֲ מַ רַ ה 'she said' I:31.

5.11 Occasional Western forms

As already pointed out (#0.1), BJA is an Eastern dialect. One of the characteristic differences between Eastern and Western Aramaic is in the masculine plural of nouns: in the West it ends in <u>ayyā</u>; in the East it ends in <u>ē</u>, #0.2. Thus, forms like חַ כַ"מַ יַ א I:33, or פַ רֹ גַ'ַ'ַ יַ א IV:77, can be easily detected as occasional Western forms.

5.12 Suffixes to plural forms

The 3rd masculine singular suffix when attached to the 3rd masculine plural verbal form may assume the form הִ וּ , הַ , or הִ' . Examples: חַ בֵ אֹ וּ הִ 'they bound him' I:31; בַ דַ קֹ וּ הַ 'they examined it' T:49; פַ דֹ י וּ הִ 'they struck him' III:78. For the form

30

·| ɔ·| 'ฏ /כ 'they brought him' I:31, see #4.7.

5.13 Aphel imperfect

The 3rd masculine singular <u>Aphel</u> imperfect of a strong verb is
either ठ८ɲּ or ठ८ɲठ . The 3rd masculine plural form is
either ·ठ८ɲּ or ·ठ८ɲठ . The doubly weak verb ເɔເ 'to come'
(#4.7) forms its <u>Aphel</u> imperfect as follows:

IV:76	'ฏ''ּ	3rd masculine singular
I:34	'| ฏ 'ּ	3rd masculine plural

5.14 Qal imperfect of Pe Aleph verbs

The following imperfect <u>Qal</u> forms of the <u>Pe Aleph</u> verbs ɲNເ 'to
say' and ठsເ 'to go' are found in the Corpus:

IV:105 ठ'ง'ּ & ठ'ง'ठ	I:34	ເຝN'ठ	3rd masculine singular
	IV:2	ເຝN'ฏ	2nd masculine singular
	IV:10	ເຝN'ເ	1st common singular

Chapter 6

BABA BATHRA 58a
lines 34-50

אמרי

34 הואיל ורהבים כולי האי ליתיב אבבא   ונידן דינא חזא דהוה כתיב באבולא כל 35

36 דין דמתקרי לדין לא שמיה דיין אמר להו אלא מעתה אתא איניש מעלמא

37ומזמן (*להו) לדינא פסליה אלא כל דין

38דמתקרי לדין ומפקן מיניה ממונא בדין

39לאו שמיה דיין כתבו הכי ברם סאבי

40דיהודאי אמרי כל דין דמתקרי לדין ומפקן

41מיניה ממונא בדין לאו שמיה דיין חזא

42(ל)דכתיב בראש כל מותאאנא דסבראש כל

43חיין אנא חמר אלא מעתה דנפיל מאיגרא

44ומית ורנפיל מריקלא ומית דמא קטליה ותו

45מן דדרכיה למימת משקן ליה חמרא וחי

46אלא הבי בעי למכתב בראש כל מרעין אנא

47דם בראש כל אסוון אנא חמר כתבו הכי

48ברם סאבי דיהודאי אמרי בראש כל מרעין

49אנא דם בראש כל אסוון אנא חמר באתר

50דלית חמר תמן מתבעו סמין

6.1 Qal imperfect of Pe Yod & Ayin Waw verbs

Forms of the 3rd masculine imperfect Qal of Pe Yod and Ayin Waw
verbs which occur in the Corpus are: Pe Yod יֵתֵ'בֿ I:35,
יֵתֵ'בֿ III:59; Ayin Waw נֵיﬞדוּן I:35.

6.2 Absolute case II

The presence of the absolute case is sometimes an indication of
an older stratum of Aramaic (see also #0.7 & #5.6). It is thus
found in quotations from an earlier era. Examples:

כָּל דַּיָּן דְּאִתְּקְרֵי לְדִין לָא שְׁמֵיה דַּיָּן

33

"any judge who is sued in court is not a judge" I:35-36;
גְּרַ֫אכֵ כַּ֫ף מַ֫ן אֵ֫סְכַ אֱמַ֫ר "at the head of all life am I,
wine" I:42-43.

6.3 Ithpeal active participle

The Ithpeal, corresponding to the Hebrew Hithpael, is the reflexive
conjugation of the Qal. For example, Qal קְרָא 'to call', Ithpeal
אֶתְקְרִי 'is called' I:36. When the נ of the prefix drops out
it is compensated by a dagesh in the first root letter, e.g
אֶתְקַטֵּל > אֶקַּטֵּל . The paradigm forms of the active participle
of the strong verb are:

אֶקַּטֵּל	masculine singular
אֶקַּטֵּלָא	feminine singular
אֶקַּטֵּלִי	masculine plural
אֶקַּטֵּלָן	feminine plural

Forms of the active participle Ithpeal which appear in the Corpus
are:

	LAMED YOD		STRONG	
I:36	אֶתְקְרִי	II:13	אֶמְסַב	masculine singular
I:50	אֶתְצַבַּר	IV:62	אֶקַּטְּרִין	masculine plural
I:50v.	אֶתְצַבָּן			feminine plural

6.4 Rhetorical questions

Frequently rhetorical questions must be deduced from context.
However, one is very often aided by the fact that the rhetorical
form, taken literally, is difficult syntactically. Examples:
אֵנָש כֹּל אִיצֵי לְמֵאן וּבֵעָן [:] פְסַלֵיהּ
"Any person could come and sue him---has he disqualified him?"
[literally, "he has disqualified him"] I:36-37;
בְּפַלָג אֶתְקְרִי וּמִית אֵנָש הַקְטֵל דְּמֵיהּ
"One who falls from a palm tree and dies---has the blood killed
him?" [literally, "the blood has killed him"] I:44;

34

אֵין מַשְׁקִין אֹתוֹ יַיִן "מִי שֶׁנִּגְמַר דִּינוֹ וְכוּ׳"

"When one is on the point of death---do they give him wine to
drink so that he will live?" [literally, "they give him wine etc."]
I:45.

6.5 Hypothetical clauses

The perfect and the participle may be used in hypothetical clauses.
Examples: כָּל אָדָם [:]בָּא וּמְעַרְעֵר עָלָיו "Any person
could come and sue him" I:36-37; הַנּוֹפֵל מִן הַגַּג וָמֵת
"One who falls from a roof and dies" I:43-44.

6.6 Independent pronouns

The independent personal pronouns have three cases: a nominative,
'I', 'you', 'he' etc.; a dative, 'to me', 'to you', 'to him' etc.;
a possessive, 'mine', 'yours', 'his' etc. The forms of the nominative are:

	PLURAL		SINGULAR		
	אֲנַן	I:42		אֲנָא	1st common
	אַתּוּן	IV:61		אַתְּ	2nd common
III:18	אִינוּן	III:11		הוּא	3rd masculine
	אִנְּהוּ	III:80 נִיהוּ	נִיהוּ אֵיהוּ		
	אִינֵּי	אֵיהִי		הִיא	3rd feminine
	נִיהֵי			נִיהִי	

6.7 Qal perfect of Ayin Waw and Ayin Yod verbs

The 3rd masculine singular perfect of the <u>Ayin Waw</u> verb קוּם 'to
get up' is קָם II:8; of the <u>Ayin Yod</u> verb מִית 'to die' it is
מִית I:44.

6.8 <u>Qal passive participle of Lamed Yod verbs</u>

Forms of the <u>Qal</u> passive participle (#3.3) of <u>Lamed Yod</u> verbs
which first occur in the Corpus are:

    I:46 'is sought'   בָּעֵי   masculine singular

    V:32 'is taught'   תַּלְיָא   feminine singular

Chapter 7

SHABBAT 156b
lines 3-18

```
3   ומדשמואל נמי אין מזל
4   לישראל דשמואל ואבלט הוו יתבי והוו
5   קאזלי הנך אינשי לאגמא א"ל אבלט
6   לשמואל האי גברא אזיל ולא אתי טריק
7   ליה חויא ומיית א"ל שמואל אי בר ישראל
8   הוא אזיל ואתי ואיתבי אזיל ואתי קם
9   אבלט שדיה לטוניה אשכח ביה חויא
10  דפסיק ושדי בתרתי גובי א"ל שמואל מאי
11  עבדת א"ל כל יומא הוה מרמינן ריפתא
12  בהדי הדדי ואכלינן האידנא הוה איכא חד
13  מינן דלא הוה ליה ריפתא הוה קא מיכסף
14  אמינא להו אנא קאימנא וארמינא כי מטאי
15  לגביה שואי נפשאי כמאן דשקילי מיניה כי
16  היכי דלא ליכסיף א"ל מצוה עבדת "נפק
17  שמואל ודרש "וצדקה תציל ממות ולא»
18  ממיתה משונה אלא ממיתה עצמה
```

7.0 Independent pronoun as copula

The 3rd person independent pronoun (#6.6) may be used as a copula
with verbal force. Examples: הוּא אִי יִשְׂרָאֵל בַּר "if he is a Jew"
II:7-8; הוּא מַלְכָּא דַּגְזֵרָא "it is the king's decree" IV:28.

7.1 Paradigm of the Qal perfect

The paradigm of the perfect of the strong verb in the Qal conjugation is as follows:

	PLURAL		SINGULAR	
				3rd masculine
				3rd feminine
				2nd masculine
				2nd feminine
				1st common

The first occurrences of these forms in the Corpus are:

	PLURAL		SINGULAR	
I:28		I:21		3rd masculine
III:12				
		I:31		3rd feminine
		I:31		
		II:11		2nd masculine
		II:26		2nd feminine
		III:17		1st common

7.2 Participle with enclitics II

In #3.9, use of the singular participle with the 1st person
enclitic was discussed. The plural participle may similarly
be joined to a shortened form of the 1st person plural pronoun
as follows: [ ] + [ ] = [ ] cf., [ ] II:12.
In other conjugations the participle may likewise be joined to
the enclitics. In the Pael, the singular participle plus enclitic
is [ ] cf., [ ] IV:107; the plural participle
plus enclitic is [ ] . In the Aphel, the singular participle
plus enclitic is [ ] cf., [ ] [:] II:14, and [ ]
III:4; the plural participle plus enclitic is [ ] cf.,
[ ] II:11.

7.3 Perfect of [ ] with the active participle II

The use of the perfect of [ ] with the active participle was
described in #1.12. Note that congruence is not always necessary

38

between the two forms, that is, they may be of different gender or number. For example, הֲוֵינָא זָרְקִין (קָרְסָא) בַּהֲדָדֵי פָּכָּא "we used to cast (our) bread together" II:11-12.

7.4 Perfect of הוי with אִיכָּא

The perfect of הוי , הֲוָה 'was', may be augmented by the form אִיכָּא 'there is', 'there are' to denote existence in the past. For example, הֲוָה אִיכָּא חַד אֵינָשׁ בֵּינַן דְּלָא הֲוָה לֵיהּ רִיפְתָּא "there was amongst us one who did not have any bread" II:12-13.

7.5 Lack of congruence with 3rd masculine singular perfect

When a verb heads the sentence it may be placed in the masculine singular regardless of the gender or number of the subject. In other words, congruence is not necessary when the masculine singular verb comes first. Examples: לָא הֲוָה לֵיהּ רִיפְתָּא "he did not have bread" II:13; נָח דַּעְתֵּיהּ "he calmed down" IV:45; חֲלַשׁ דַּעְתֵּיהּ "he was upset" IV:102; נָח נַפְשֵׁיהּ "he died" IV:104; פַּג דַּעְתֵּיהּ "he lost consciousness" IV:109.

7.6 1st person perfect of Lamed Aleph/Yod verbs

As can be seen from the paradigm in #7.1, the form of the 1st person singular perfect of the strong verb is קָטְלִי . With Lamed Aleph and Lamed Yod verbs the 1st person ending is with ay, not ī. Thus, from מַטֵא 'to reach', מַטַאי 'I reached' II:14. Similarly, in the Pael conjugation, instead of the ending ī of the strong verb, e.g. שַׁדְּרִי 'I sent', we find ay, e.g. שַׁוַּאִי [נַשַׁוַּאִי +] 'I pretended' II:15.

7.7 Pronoun used as conjunction

The pronoun מַאן 'who', when used relatively, e.g. 'as one who' may have the sense of the conjunction 'if' or 'though', e.g. 'as if' or 'as though'. For example,
שַׁוַּאִי נַפְשַׁאי כְּמַאן דְּשַׁדַּר' [לְקַטֵל :text] אֵינָשׁ

39

"I pretended as if I had taken [text: were taken] from him" II:15.

7.8 Other forms of the Ithpeal (#6.3)

The 3rd masculine singular perfect of the Ithpeal conjugation of
a strong verb is אתקטל ; the imperfect form is יתקטל ; the
imperative is אתקטל. Forms of the perfect, imperfect, and
imperative Ithpeal which appear in the Corpus are:

Perfect

	LAMED YOD		STRONG	
II:23	אתגלי	III:73	אתקצע	3rd masculine singular
III:9	אתבני	IV:35	אתפנאו	
		V:37	אצרב	
III:91	אתבעי			3rd feminine singular
		IV:10v.	אתקטלתון	2nd masculine plural

Imperfect

		II:16	יתכסו	3rd masculine singular

Imperative

		IV:10v.	אתקטלו	masculine plural

40

Chapter 8

SHABBAT 156b
lines 18-37

ומדר״ע

18 נמי אין מזל לישראל דר״ע הויא ליה ברתא 19

20 אמרי ליה כלדאי ההוא יומא דעיילה לבי

21 גננא טריק לה חויא ומיתא הוה דאיגא

22 אמילתא טובא ההוא יומא שקלתה

23 למכבנתא דצתא בגודא איתרמי איתיב

24 בעיניה דחויא לצפרא כי קא שקלה לה

25 הוה קא סריך ואתי חויא בתרה אמר לה

26 אבוה מאי עבדת אמרה ליה בפניא אתא

27 עניא קרא אבבא והו טרידי כולי עלמא

28 בסעודתא וליכא דשמעיה קאימנא שקלתי

29 (לה)*לריסתנאי דיהבית לי יהבתיה ניהליה אמר

30 לה מצוה עבדת נפק ר״ע ודרש וצדקה תציל

31 ממות ולא ממיתה משונה אלא ממיתה

32 עצמה ומדר״נ בר יצחקנמי אין מזל לישראל

33 דאימיה דר״נ בר יצחק אמרי לה כלדאי בריך גנבא הוה לא שבקתיה גלויי

34 רישיה אמרה ליה יכסי רישיך כי היכי דתיהוו עלך אימתא דשמיא ובעי

35 רחמי לא הוה ידע אמאי קאמרה ליה יומא חד יתיב קא גריס תותי

36 דיקלא נפל גלימא מעילויה רישיה דלי עיניה חזא לדיקלא אלמיה יצריה

37 סליק פסקיה לקיבורא בשיניה:

8.1 Paradigm of Qal perfect of Lamed Aleph/Yod verbs

The paradigm of the perfect Qal of Lamed Aleph and Lamed Yod
verbs consists mostly of forms which occur in the Corpus.

41

PLURAL	SINGULAR		
I:22 קֵוּי	I:5 נְקַא I:5 קְדָן		3rd masculine
	II:36 קֵל		
חֵלֵקּאִ	III:91 קֵבוּת II:19 קִ׳נְ׳ק		3rd feminine
חֵלֵין	IV:102 אֵנּאק		
		חֵלֵ׳ת	2nd masculine
חֵלֵ׳תוּן	IV:4 לֵבּת		
חֵלֵן	II:14 נְקַוּאִ		1st common

8.2 Alternate form of the passive participle

Just as there is an alternate form for the masculine singular
active participle (#4.8), so there is an alternate form for the
masculine singular passive participle (#3.3). Thus, alongside
קְטִיל is found קְטִילַא or קְטִילָה, e.g. בְּקַא 'worried' II:21.

8.3 3rd person suffix to the 3rd feminine singular

The 3rd feminine singular Qal perfect form is קַטְלַא or קַטְלָה,
#5.10. With the 3rd masculine singular suffix it assumes the form
קַטְלֵהּ, and with the 3rd feminine singular suffix it is קַטְלַתַּהּ.
Examples: שְׁקַלְתֵּהּ "she took it" II:22; לָא שַׁבְקַתֵּהּ "she did not
permit him" II:33. The form בְּצוּק in II:23 possibly should be
read בְּצַתַּהּ, and be taken as a 3rd feminine suffix to the 3rd feminine singular of the Ayin Waw root צוּב, with the meaning 'she
stuck it'.

8.4 Qal perfect of Pe Yod verbs

Forms of the perfect Pe Yod Qal which appear in the Corpus are:

II:23	אִיתֵב	3rd masculine singular
II:29v.	יְדַבְתְּ	2nd masculine singular
[text: יְדַבְתְּ]		
III:52	יְתֵבוּ	3rd masculine plural
III:86	יְתֵבוּ	

42

8.5 Circumstantial clauses

A circumstantial clause is one which indicates the circumstances
or condition of the subject of a main clause. Examples: the
phrase וְכַ֫וֵּי 'ﬠֵיﬞﬞ in בְּﬠִבִﬞﬞﬞﬞﬞﬞﬞﬞﬞﬞﬞﬞﬞﬞ
"he called at the gate while everyone was busy with the meal" II:
27-28; and the phrase הָ֫וﬞ בָּכְיָﬞﬞ in   אַבְﬥﬞﬞﬞ אַחֲﬞﬞﬞﬞ הָ֫וﬞ בָּכְיָﬞﬞ
"his sister came crying" IV:102-103.

8.6 3rd masculine suffix to 1st person singular

Two examples of the 3rd masculine suffix to the 1st person singular
perfect occur in the Corpus. One is in the <u>Qal</u>, יְהַבְﬨֵּהּ "I gave
it" II:29, and the other in the <u>Aphel</u>, אַזְמִנְﬨֵּהּ "I invited him"
III:89.

8.7 Dative personal pronouns

Only two forms of the dative personal pronouns (#6.6) appear in
the Corpus: נִיהֲֵ֫לָ֫ך 'to you' III:67; and נִיהֲלֵהּ 'to him' II:29.

8.8 Casus pendens

In a casus pendens [literally, a 'hanging' or 'dangling' case] the
subject is first introduced, and then referred back to by a pronominal suffix. For example, אִמֵּיהּ דְּרַ֫ב נַחְמָן בַּר יִﬥ֫חָק אָמְﬞﬞﬞ ﬥﬞﬞ כַּﬥְﬞﬞﬞﬞ
literally, "Rabbi Nachman bar Yizhaq's mother, astrologers told
her" = "astrologers told Rabbi Nachman bar Yizhaq's mother" II:33.

8.9 Infinitive without לְ

The infinitive (#3.2) is normally preceded by the preposition לְ .
Sometimes, however, the לְ can be omitted as, for example, in
לָא שָׁבְקָﬞﬞ לֵיהּ גַּﬥֵּﬞﬞ ﬞﬞ "she did not permit him to uncover his
head" II:33-34. Note that the infinitive of the <u>Pael</u> is קַֻﬞﬞﬞﬞﬞ ,
#3.10.

43

8.10 Imperative of weak verbs

The imperative of the strong verb is קְטֹל , #2.11, #5.5. With
the weak verbs it assumes the following forms:

Pe Aleph	אֱ'ס	#2.11
Pe Yod	רֵד	III:70
Ayin Waw	קוּם	III:85
Double Ayin	צֹר	IV:29
Lamed Yod	בְּצַי	II:34
Pe Aleph & Lamed Aleph	מְלִא	IV:28

The <u>Pael</u> imperative of a strong verb is קַטֵּל , and of a <u>Lamed
Yod</u> verb is like בַּסִּי II:34.

8.11 Imperfect Qal of Lamed Yod verbs

Forms of the imperfect <u>Qal</u> of <u>Lamed Yod</u> verbs which appear in the
Corpus are:

III:52	יִקְצֵי	3rd masculine singular
IV:36	יִקְרֵי	
III:23	יִקְצֵוּן	3rd masculine plural
IV:88	יִקְרוּ	
II:34	תִּקְרֶינָּה	3rd feminine plural

8.12 Intransitive verbs

Intransitive verbs are those verbs which do not take a direct
object. Whereas transitive verbs assume a form קַטֵּל in the perfect
and יִקְטֹלוּ or יִקְטֹל in the imperfect, intransitive verbs form
their perfect like קָטֵל , e.g. עָלֹה 'he went up' II:37, and form
their imperfect either like יִקְטֵל or like יִקְטַל , cf., יֶאֱסֹר
IV:28.

44

Chapter 9

SANHEDRIN 108b-109a
lines a-19

‏*נחום איש גם‏

a

‏bזוהוה רגיל דכל דהוה סלקא ליה אמר גם זו לטובה יומא חד בעו [ישראל] לשדורי דורון לקיסר אמרי בהדי‏

‏1מאן נשדר נשדר בהדי נחום איש גם זו‏
‏2דמלומד בנסים הוא כי מטא ההוא דיורא‏
‏3בעא למיבת אמרי ליה מאי איכא בהדך‏
‏4אמר להו קא מובילנא כרגא לקיסר קמו‏
‏5בליליא שרינהו לסיפטיה ושקלו כל דהוה‏
‏6גביה ומלנהו עפרא כי מטא להתם אישתכח‏
‏7עפרא אמר אחוכי קא מחייכי בי יהודאי‏
‏8אפקוהו למקטליה אמר גם זו לטובה אתא‏
‏9אליהו ואידמי להו כחד מינייהו אמר להו‏
‏10דילמא האי עפרא מעפרא דאברהם אבינו‏
‏11הוא דהוה שדי עפרא הוו חרבי נילי הוו נירי‏
‏12בדוק ואשכחו הכי הוה מחווא דלא הוו קא‏
‏13יכלי ליה למיכבשיה שרו מההוא עפרא‏
‏14עליה וכבשוה עיילוהו לבי גנזא אמרי שקול‏
‏15דניחא לך מלייה לסיפטא דהבא כי הדר‏
‏16אתא אמרו ליה הנך דיורי מאי אמטית לבי‏
‏17מלכא אמר להו מאי דשקלי מהכא אמטאי‏
‏18להתם שקלי אינהו אמטו להתם קטלינהו‏
‏19להנך דיורי :‏

In this chapter a small section of Taanit 21a is used for comparison with the Sanhedrin text. Its forms are identified by the letter T followed by the appropriate line number.

*ו#אמאי קרו ליה נחום איש גם זו דכל מילתא דהוה סלקא 40
41 ליה אמר גם זו לטובה *זימנא הדא בעו לשדורי ישראל דורון לבי קיסר אמרו מאן ייזיל ייזיל נחום איש גם זו
42 דמלומד בניסין הוא שדרו בידיה מלא סיפטא דאבנים טובות ומרגליות אזל בת בההוא דירה בליליא קמו הנך
43 דיוראי ושקלינהו לסיפטיה ומלונהו עפרא [למדר כי חזנהו אמר גם זו לטובה) כי מטא התם [שרינהו לסיפטא
44 חזנהו דמלו עפרא] בעא מלכא למקטלינהו לכולהו אמר קא מחייכו בי יהודאי [אמר גם זו לטובה] אתא אליהו
45 אדמי ליה כחד מיניהו א"ל דלמא הא עפרא מעפרא דאברהם אבוהון הוא דכי הוה שרי עפרא הוו סיפיה
46 גילי הוו גירי דכתיב °יתן כעפר חרבו כקש נדף קשתו הויא חדא מדינתא דלא מצו למיכבשה בדקו מיניה
47 ובבשיה עיילו לבי גנויה ומלוהו לסיפטיה אבנים טובות ומרגליות ושדרוהו ביקרא רבה כי אתו ביתו בההוא
48 דירה אמרו ליה מאי אייתית בהרך דעבדי לך יקרא כולי האי אמר להו מאי דשקלי מהכא אמטי להתם סתרו
49 לדירייהו ואמטינהו לבי מלכא אמרו ליה האי עפרא דאייתי הכא מדידן הוא בדקוה ולא אשבחוה וקטלינהו להנך
50 דיוראי :

9.1 Imperfect Pael

The 3rd person imperfect <u>Pael</u> of the strong verb is either יְקַטֵּל
or יְקַטֵל. Examples יְסַפַר III:1; תְֿפֶֿקֶֿד III:87.

9.2 Aphel of Pe Yod verbs

In the <u>Aphel</u> conjugation of <u>Pe Yod</u> verbs the initial <u>yod</u> becomes
<u>waw</u>. For example, the <u>Aphel</u> forms of the verb יְתֵב 'to sit'
are: perfect, אוֹתֵיב, imperfect, נוֹתֵיב, and participle מוֹתֵיב.
Examples in the Corpus are: אַיְבֵּי 'bringing' III:4, and מוֹתְבָא
'making sit' IV:54.

9.3 Qal paradigm of Ayin Waw/Yod verbs

Forms of the <u>Ayin Waw</u> and <u>Ayin Yod</u> verbs which appear in the Corpus
are:

I:44	מִית	3rd masculine singular
II:8	קָם	
III:85	מִיתַת	3rd feminine singular
III:4	קָמוּ	3rd masculine plural
T:47	גָּבוּ	

46

9.4 3rd masculine plural suffix

The 3rd masculine plural suffix הוֹן (#2.5) becomes נְהוֹן when
attached to verbal forms. With the 3rd masculine singular
perfect the forms which occur in the Corpus are:

קְטַלִינֹהוּ	'he killed them'	III:52
שְׁקַלִינֹהוּ	'he took them'	III:52
חַזַנֹהוּ	'he saw them'	T:43

With the 3rd masculine plural perfect the forms which occur in the
Corpus are:

קְטַלִינֹהוּ	'they killed them'	III:18; T:49
שְׁקַלִינֹהוּ	'they took them'	T:43
מְלַנֹהוּ	'they filled them'	III:6
מְלוֹנֹהוּ	'they filled them'	T:43
שְׁרִינֹהוּ	'they untied them'	III:5; T:43
חַזַנֹהוּ	'they saw them'	T:44
אַיְתֹנֹהוּ	'they brought them'	T:49

9.5 Ithpaal conjugation

The Ithpaal conjugation, like the Ithpeal (#6.3), corresponds to
the Hebrew Hithpael, and is the reflexive conjugation of the Pael.
The paradigm forms are: perfect, אִתְקַטֵּל , imperfect, יִתְקַטֵּל , &
participle, מִתְקַטֵּל . It is very difficult to distinguish the
Ithpaal from the Ithpeal in form especially in an unpointed text
like BJA. For example, אִתְכְּתְבָה 'it was found' III:6 could be
either Ithpeal אִתְכְּנַתָה or Ithpaal אִתְכַּתְבָה . The general rule is
that the reflexive form is Ithpaal if the verb in its active
meaning occurs in the Pael. Thus, מִצְטַעַר 'he was grieving'
IV:104 is Ithpaal because the Pael, and not the Qal, has the
active meaning 'to grieve'. On the other hand, אִתֹּקֹן 'be afraid
of' IV:89 is Ithpeal, because the verb has no Pael. Forms of the
Ithpaal which occur in the Corpus are:

Perfect

III:6 [?]	אוֹקְתֵּ֫בַ ח	3rd masculine singular
V:38	אוֹק֫בְּי	
IV:75	אוֹקְתְּ֫רֵי׳	1st common singular

Participle

IV:104	מְ֫קַ֫ג֫צַר	masculine singular
V:80	מְ֫קַ֫בְּדָא	feminine singular

Imperfect III:67   יְ֫צַבַּ֫ה   3rd masc sing + 3rd fem
suffix

9.6 Aphel infinitive

The Aphel infinitive is אַקְ֫גִל , e.g. אַקְ֫יִם IV:32; אַקְ֫נִבְ III:7; אַ֫רְ֫יִ׳ IV:98. The infinitives of the active conjugations are thus:

QAL   מְקַ֫גֹל
PAEL   קַ֫גִּ׳
APHEL   אַקְ֫גִּ׳

Remember that the infinitive is often used with the finite form of the verb for emphasis (#3.4)

9.7 Infinitive with suffixes

The suffixes are attached to the Qal infinitive as follows:

3rd masculine singular suffix   מְקַ֫גְלֵה   'to kill him' III:8
3rd feminine singular suffix   מְ֫כַבְּדָה   'to conquer it' T:46
3rd masculine plural suffix   מְקַ֫גֹל'(נְ)הוֹן   'to kill them' T:44

An example of a suffix to a Pael infinitive is שְֽׁזָבוּתֵ֫ה 'to save him' IV:46.

9.8 Aphel perfect of Lamed Aleph/Yod verbs

Forms of the Aphel perfect of Lamed Aleph and Lamed Yod verbs which appear in the Corpus are:

48

I:20	אׄיׄ"ׄתׄ'	3rd masculine singular
III:16	אׄיׄןׄ ׄ'תׄ	2nd masculine singular
T:48	אׄיׄ"ׄתׄ'ׄ תׄ	
III:17	אׄיׄןׄ ׄאׄיׄ	1st common singular
III:18	אׄיׄ ׄ ׄיׄ	3rd masculine plural
III:87	אׄיׄתׄ'ׄ	

9.9 The form נׄ'תׄא

The form נׄ'תׄא in III:15 is a feminine singular passive participle
(#3.3) of the Ayin Waw verb נׄוׄח . The masculine singular of this
type of verb is נׄ'ח or נׄ'תׄ . The phrase בׄ'נׄ'תׄא לׄבׄ means
"whatever is pleasing to you," "whatever you want."

9.10 Occasional Western forms II

Since one of the major differences between Eastern and Western
Aramaic is in the prefix of the imperfect (#0.2), the form יׄזׄל
'he will go' T:41, instead of the expected נׄזׄל or לׄזׄל
(#5.14), can easily be detected as a Western form. See also #5.11.

9.11 Possessive personal pronouns

The following forms of the possessive personal pronouns (#6.6)
appear in the Corpus: דׄיׄלׄי 'mine' III:82; דׄיׄלׄך 'yours' V:85;
דׄיׄלׄה 'his' III:87; דׄיׄלׄן 'ours' T:49.

Chapter 10

SANHEDRIN 109a-109b
lines 51-93

51 אמרי *דאית ליה חד תורא מרעי חד יומא דלית ל

52 לירעי תרי יומי ההוא ירמא בר ארמלתא הבו ליה תורי למרעיה אזל שקלינהו וקטלינהו אמר ל

53 *דאית ליה תורא נשקול חד משכא דלית

54 ליה תורא נשקול תרי משכי אמרו ליה מאי

55 האי אמר להו סוף דינא כתחילת דינא מה

56 תחילת דינא דאית ליה תורא מרעי חד יומא

57 דלית ליה תורי מרעי תרי יומי אף סוף דינא

58 דאית ליה חד תורא לשקול חד דלית ליה

59 תורא לשקול תרי דעבר במברא ניתיב חד

60 זוזא דלא עבר במברא ניתיב תרי דהוה ליה

61 (תורא) [דרא] דלבני אתי כל חד והד שקל

62 חדא א"ל אנא חדא דשקלי דהוה שדי תומי

63 או שמכי אתו כל חד והד שקיל חדא א"ל

64 אנא חדא דשקלי ארבע דייני הוו בסדום

65 שקראי ושקרוראי זייפי ומצלי דינא דמחי

66 ליה לאיתתא דהברי' ומפלא ליה אמרי ליה

67 יהבה ניהליה דניעברה ניהליך דפסיק ליה

68 לאודנא דחמרא דהבריה אמרו ליה הבה

69 ניהליה עד דקדחא דפדע ליה לחבריה

70 אמרי ליה הב ליה אגרא דשקל לך דמא

71 דעבר במברא יהיב ארבעה זוזי דעבר

72 במיא יהיב תמני זווי זימנא חדא אתא ההוא

73 כובס איקלע להתם אמרו ליה הב ד' זווי

74 אמר להו אנא במיא עברי אמרו ליה א"כ

75 הב תמניא דעברת במיא לא יהיב פדיוהי

76 אתא לקמיה דדיינא א"ל הב ליה אגרא

77 דשקיל לך דמא ותמניא זוזי דעברת במיא

78 אליעזר עבד אברהם איתרמי התם פדיוהי

79 אתא לקמיה דינא א"ל הב ליה אגרא

80 דשקל לך דמא שקל גללא פדיוהי איהו

81 לדיינא אמר מאי האי א"ל אגרא דנפק לי

82 מינך הב ניהליה להאי ווי דידי כדקיימי

83 קיימי הוא להו פורייתא דהו מגני עלה

84 אורחין כי מאריך גייזי ליה כי גוץ מתחין ליה אליעזר עבד אברהם אקלע

להתם אמרו ליה קום נגי אפוריא אמר להון נדרא נדרי מן יומא דמיתת אמא לא גנינא אפוריא כי הוה מתרמי

להו עניא יהבו ליה כל חד וחד דינרא וכתיב שמיה עליה וריפתא לא הו כמטי ליה כי הוה מית אתי כל חד

וחד שקיל דידיה הכי אתני ביינהו כל מאן דמזמין גברא לבי הילולא לישלח גלימא הוי האי הילולא

אקלע אליעזר להתם ולא יהבו ליה נהמא כי בעי למסער אתא אליעזר ויתיב לסיפא דכולהו אמרו

ליה מאן אזמנך להכא א"ל ההוא א"ל [דיתיב] אתה זמנתן [אמר דילמא שמעי בי דאנא אזמנתיה ומשלחי

ליה מאניה דהאי גברא] שקל גלימיה ההוא דיתיב גביה ורהט לברא וכן עבד לכולהו עד דנפקו כולהו

ואבלא איהו לסעודתא הוא ההיא רביתא דהות קא מפקא ריפתא לעניא בחצבא אינלאי מלתא שפיוה

דובשא ואוקמה על איגר שורא אתא זיבורי ואבלוה והיינו דכתיב °ויאמר ה' זעקת סדום ועמורה כי

רבה ואמר רב יהודה אמר רב על עיסקי ריבה:

10.1 The form (form)

The form (form) III:52, consisting of an infinitive plus suffix
(#9.7), literally means 'to tend it'. But the singular suffix
does not agree with the plural noun 'תוֹרֵי' 'oxen'. Hence, it
seems to be an error for the infinitive without the suffix (form)
(#3.2) 'to tend'.

10.2 Paradigm of the imperfect Qal

The paradigm forms of the imperfect Qal of strong verbs are:

PLURAL	SINGULAR	
נ ק ט ל ·	ל ט ק נ	3rd masculine
ל ט ק ·	ל ק ט	
נ ק ט	נ ק ט ל ת	3rd feminine
ל ק ט		
· ל ק ט ת	נ ק ט ל ת	2nd masculine
· ל ק ט ת	· ל ק ט	2nd feminine
נ ק ט ל	ל ט ק א	1st common

The first occurrences of these forms in the Corpus are:

	PLURAL		SINGULAR	
IV:87	·ן ג ٰבֶל	III:53	דֿוֹן ֶֽבֿ	3rd masculine
		III:58	דֿ וֹן ֶֿבֿ	
IV:87v.	ןֿצֶֽבֿٰ			3rd feminine
		IV:29	בֿ'אָֿרֿﬦ	2nd masculine
		IV:28	בֿ'אָֿרֿ﬩	1st common

10.3 Pleonastic use of ל

The preposition ל is often used pleonastically, that is, redun-
dantly. This means that, although the preposition stands alongside
the verb, it does not modify its meaning in any way. For example,
אֿﬞל 'נֿאָֿבֿ "whoever strikes" III:65-66. It is often difficult
to tell when the preposition is being used pleonastically, or as
part of the next construction to be discussed.

10.4 Passive participle with ל

The passive participle is often used with the preposition ל with
the meaning of a perfect. The suffixes to the ל specify the
subject. Examples: 'ﬞל ﬧ'אֶֿבֿ 'I heard'; וֿﬞל ﬧ'נֿﬦ ﬧﬞ﬩﬩ "they did not
hear" V:39. Phrases such as אֿ'רֿﬞבֿٰﬦ ﬩﬩'ﬦ﬩ אֿﬞל 'נֿאָֿבٰ "whoever
struck his friend's wife" III:65-66, may be interpreted under this
heading, or as a pleonastic use of the preposition (see #10.3)
with the verb vocalized as a present participle, e.g. אֿﬞל 'נֿחָ֫בٰ .
Another example of this type is: ﬩﬩'נֿﬦﬦ ﬩﬩'﬩ﬦﬦﬞל אֿﬞל 'ן'סֶ֣בٰ
"whoever cut off the ear of his friend's donkey" III:67-68, where
we could read ן'סֶ֣בٰ or ן'סֶ֣בٰ .

10.5 Independent pronoun used for emphasis

Any independent pronoun may be used for emphasis, even though its
presence is not strictly required. Examples: ﬩﬩"אֿﬞבٰ ·ﬦﬦ'ﬦ 'ﬦ·ﬦֿבﬦ
"he [text: they] struck him, he, the judge" = "he struck the judge"
III:80-81; ﬩ﬧﬞﬦ_ﬦﬦﬦֿבٰ 'ﬦﬦﬞל 'ﬦﬦ'ﬦ ﬩ﬦﬞﬧﬧ'ﬦﬦﬦ ﬩ﬧﬦﬦ literally, "the
reader of the letter, he, let him be the messenger" = "let him who

gives advice carry it out" IV:36

10.6 Absolute case III

A further use of the absolute case is as a predicate adjective,
that is, where the adjective is used as a verb as, for example,
גַבְרָא טָב "the man is good," as opposed to גַבְרָא טָבָא "the good
man." Examples: אָגִיד 'short' in כִּי אָגִיד נְתַח לֵהּ "if he was
too short, they stretched him" III:84; שַׁפִּיר 'beautiful' in
הָבִיַּת לָךְ אַחוֹתִי דְשַׁפִּירָא מִנִּי "I will give you my sister who
is more beautiful than I" IV:98.

10.7 More suffixes

The form זַמְּנָתַן 'you invited me' III:89 has a 1st person singular
suffix attached to a 2nd person singular Pael form. The form
אַזְמְנָךְ 'he invited you' III:89 has a 2nd person singular suffix
attached to a 3rd masculine singular Aphel form. Both are from
the root זמן which means 'to invite' in the Pael and Aphel.

10.8 The form דַּכְוָתֵיהּ

The form דַּכְוָתֵיהּ 'it corresponds to', 'it is this' III:92 is tra-
ditionally vocalized דַּכְוָתֵיהּ. However, because it is made up of
דְּכֵין (masculine demonstrative pronoun, #3.5) plus הוּא (personal
pronoun), it should be vocalized דַּכְוָתֵיהּ.

Chapter 11

BABA MEZIA 83a-83b
lines 1-36

1   **גמ׳** פשיטא לא צריכא

2 ⁱדטפא לתו אאגרייתו מהו דתימא אמר לתו הא דטפאי לתו

3 אאגרייכו אדעתא דמקדמיתו ומחשביתו בהדאי קא משמע לן דאמרו

4 ליה האי דטפת לן אדעתא דעבדינן לך עבידתא שפירתא אמר ריש לקיש

5 ⁱⁱפועל בכניסתו משלו ביציאתו משל בעל

     הבית שנאמר °תזרח השמש יאספון ואל

     מעונתם ירבצון יצא אדם לפעלו ולעבודתו

     עדי ערב וליחזי היכי ⁱⁱבעיר הדשה

     וניחזי מהיכא קא אתו בנקוטאי איבעית

10 אימא דאמר לתו ⁱⁱדאגריתו לי כפועל

     דאורייתא דרש רבי זירא ואמרי לה תני רב

     יוסף מאי דכתיב °תשת חשך ויהי לילה בו

     תרמוש כל חיתו יער תשת חשך ויהי לילה

     זה *העולם הוה שדומה ללילה בו תרמוש

15 כל חיתו יער אלו רשעים שבו שדומין לחיה

     שביער תזרח השמש יאספון ואל מעונתם

     ירבצון תזרחהשמש לצדיקים יאספן רשעים

     לגיהנם ואל מעונתם ירבצון *אין לך כל

     צדיק וצדיק שאין לו מדור לפי כבודו יצא

20 אדם לפעלו יצאו צדיקים לקבל שכרן

     ולעבודתו עדי ערב במי שהשלים עבודתו

     עדי ערב ר׳ אלעזר ב״ר שמעון אשבח

     לההוא פרהגונא דקא תפיס גנבי אמר ליה

     היכי יכלת לתו לאו כחיותא מתילי דכתיב

25 בו תרמוש כל חיתו יער איכא דאמרי מהאי

     קרא קאמר ליה °יארב במסתר כאריה*בסוכו

     דלמא שקלת צדיקי ושבקת רשיעי א״ל ומai

     אעביד הרמנאדמל׳כא הואאמר(⁶)תא אנמרך

     היכי תעביד עול בארבע שעי לחנותא כי

30 חזית איניש דקא שתי חמרא וקא נקיט כסא

31 בידיה וקא מנמנם שאול עילויה אי צורבא
מרבנן הוא וניים אקרומי קדים לגרסיה אי
33 פועל הוא קדים קא עביד עבידתיה ואי
עבידתיה בליליא רדוי רדיד ואי לא גנבא
35 הוא ותפסיה אישתמע מילתא בי מלכא
אמר *קרײנא דאיגרתא איהו ליהוי פרונקא

11.1 Rhetorical phrases I

Many phrases, especially in the legal sections of the Talmud,
are often employed rhetorically. Their precise meaning can only
be determined by the context. As will be seen, some of the much
used phrases are actually Hebrew. The rhetorical phrases which
occur in this section are:

פְּשִׁיטָא לאֹ צְרִיכָא   IV:1 lit. "it is plain, no! it is necessary"
= "is it not obvious? no! it is necessary to state it"

מָהוּ דְּתֵימָא   IV:2 lit. "what is it you might think" =
"you might think that"

קָמַשְׁמַע לָן   IV:3 lit. "he teaches us" = "we are
taught"

הֵיכִי דָמֵי   IV:8 lit. "how are they accustomed?" =
"what is the custom?"

אִיבָּעֵית   IV:9 lit. "if you wish" = "alternatively,"
"if you prefer another solution"

אֵימָא   IV:10 lit. "I will say" = "I might suppose"

11.2 Feminine nouns understood

In the phrase פְּשִׁיטָא לאֹ צְרִיכָא , the forms פְּשִׁיטָא and צְרִיכָא are
feminine singular passive participles. They are feminine because
they are understood to refer to a feminine subject. Similarly,
in the rhetorical phrase שָׁמַע מִינַהּ literally, "he understood from
it" = "he inferred that" IV:44, the feminine suffix on מִינַהּ must
refer to an understood feminine subject. The feminine subject will
vary according to circumstances, but the most common are: מִילְּתָא

56

'word', אֲמַ֫רְנָא 'a mishnah', מַתְנִיתִין 'the Mishnah' (lit.,
'our mishnah') V:49, & בָּרַיְתָא 'Baraitha' V:42.

11.3 Participle with enclitics III

We have seen that the active participle may be joined to the lst
person singular (#3.9), and the lst person plural (#7.2) enclitics.
It can also, like the passive participle (#5.2) be joined to the
2nd person enclitics as follows:

Singular   הָזֵ֫ית =   אַתְּ + הָזֵ֫

     cf., בָּ֫זַת IV:24;   בָּעֵ֫ית IV:9 (אַתְּ + בָּעֵ֫)

───

Plural   הָזֵיתוּן =   אַתּוּן + הָזֵ֫

     cf., אַ֫כְלִיתוּן IV:10

Pael   מְהַזֵיתוּן =   אַתּוּן + מְהַזֵ֫

     cf., מְחַ֫פְאַתּוּן IV:3; מְסַבְּרִיתוּן IV:3

11.4 The form אַגְ֫רִיתוּן

The form אַגְ֫רִיתוּן in IV:10 is an active participle masculine plural
plus the 2nd person plural enclitic, and means "you are hiring."
The context, however, requires either a passive "you are hired,"
or an imperative "be hired!". Thus, one of the variants in the
Ithpeal conjugation, אִתַּגַּרְתּוּן perfect 2nd person plural "you are
hired," or אִתַּגַּרוּ imperative masculine plural "be hired!"
is to be preferred.

11.5 Imperfect with suffixes

The following imperfect with suffixes forms are found in the Corpus:

אַגְמְרָ֫ךְ "I will teach you" IV:28, a 2nd masculine singular suffix
to a lst person Aphel singular.

נִמְלֵי֫הּ "let him fill it" IV:77, a 3rd masculine singular suffix to a 3rd masculine singular <u>Pael</u>.

יְטַגְּאֵהּ "he will calm him" IV:105, a 3rd masculine singular
suffix to a 3rd masculine singular <u>Pael</u> [contextually, a feminine
suffix is expected, e.g. יְטַגְּאַהּ].

נִיתְּאֵהּ "let him place it" IV:79, a 3rd masculine singular
suffix to a 3rd masculine singular <u>Aphel</u>.

11.6 <u>Palpel conjugation</u>

The <u>Palpel</u> conjugation consists of a duplication of the first and
third root letters of an <u>Ayin Waw</u> or a <u>Double Ayin</u> verb, e.g.
from נוּם, the form נַמְנֵם . It is used instead of the <u>Pael</u>
for some, but not all (#3.7), <u>Ayin Waw</u> and <u>Double Ayin</u> verbs, e.g.
נַמְנֵם 'dozing' IV:31. The form נָ''ם IV:32 is not a <u>Pael</u>, but
a present participle (#2.9).

11.7 <u>The phrase אֲקֵיפוּ קָפֵּיס</u>

As it stands, the phrase אֲקֵיפוּ קָפֵּיס IV:32 consists of an
<u>Aphel</u> infinitive (#9.6) plus a 3rd masculine singular <u>Pael</u> perfect
(#3.7). While it is true that infinitives go with finite verbs
for emphasis (#3.4), they must, however, be of the same conjugation
as the finite verb. Thus, the variant for קָפֵּיס, אֲקֵיפֵּיס an
<u>Aphel</u> perfect, is therefore to be preferred.

Chapter 12

BABA MEZIA 83b-84a
lines 37-74

37 אתויה לרבי אלעזר ברבי שמעון וקא תפיס
גנבי ואזיל שלח ליה ר' יהושע בן קרחה
חומץ בן יין 'עד מתי אתה מוסר עמו של
40 אלהינו להריגה שלח ליה קוצים אני מכלה
מן הכרם שלח ליה ייבא בעל הכרם ויכלה
42 את קוציו יומא חד פגע ביה ההוא כובס
קרייה חומץ בן יין אמר מדחציף כולי האי
44 שמע מינה רשיעא הוא אמר להו תפסוהו
תפסוהו לבתר דנח דעתיה אזל בתריה
46 לפרוקיה ולא מצי קרי עליה °שומר פיו
ולשונו שומר מצרות נפשו זקפוהו קם תותי
48 זקיפא וקא בכי אמרו ליה רבי *אל ירע
בעיניך שהוא ובנו בעלו נערה מאורסה ביום
50 הכפורים הניח ידו על בני מעיו אמר שישו
בני מעי שישו ומה ספיקות שלכם כך ודאית שלכם על אחת כמה וכמה
52 מובטח אני בכם שאין רמה ותולעה שולטת בכם זאפי' הכי לא מיתבא
דעתיה אשקיותו סמא דשינתא ועיילותי לביתא דשישא וקרעו לכריסיה
54 הוו מפקן מיניה דיקולי דתרבא ומתבי בשמשא בתמוז ואב
ולא מסרח כל תרבא נמי לא סריח כל תרבא לא סריח שורייק
56 סומק מסריח הכא אף על גב דאיכא שורייקי סומק לא מסריח
קרי אנפשיה °אף בשרי ישכן לבטח ואף ר' ישמעאל ברבי יוסי מטא
58 כי האי מעשה לידיה פגע ביה אליהו אמר ליה
עד מתי אתה מוסר עמו של אלהינו להריגה
60 אמר ליה מאי אעביד הרמנא דמלכא הוא אמר
ליה אבוך ערק לאסיא את ערוק ללודקיא כי
62 הוו מקלעי ר' ישמעאל ברבי יוסי ור' אלעזר
בר' שמעון בהדי הדדי הוה עייל בקרא דתורי
64 ביניידו ולא הוה נגעה בהו אמרה להו ההיא
מטרוניתא בניכם אינם שלכם אמרו להשלהן
66 גדול משלנו כל שכן איכא דאמרי הכי אמרו
לה °כי כאיש גבורתו איכא דאמרי הכי אמרו

אלה אהבה דוחקת את הבשר ולמה לתו 68
לאהדורי לה והאכתיב °אל תענכסיל כאולתו
שלא להוציא לעז על בניהם א״ר יותנן איבריה 70
דר׳ ישמעאל [בר׳ יוסי] כהמת בת תשע קבין
אמר רב פפא איבריה דרבי יותנן כהמת בת 72
חמשת קבין ואמרי לה בת שלשת קבין דרב
פפא נופיה כי דקורי דהרפנאי

12.1 Shortened form א

The letter א attached to a word may be a shortened form of the
word בַּר 'son of', as in רַבִּ׳ אֱלִיעֶזֶר אֲבָא דְּשִׁמְעוֹן "Rabbi Eliezer,
son of Rabbi Simeon" IV:37. It may also represent a shortened
form of the word אֲ׳ (construct of בֵּיתָא), literally, 'of the
house of' = 'of the school of'.

12.2 Auxiliary use of אָזֵל

The participle אָזֵל may be used as an auxiliary 'going to',
'proceeding to'. It may stand before the verb, as in הֲוָה קָא אָזֵל
וְקָרַע אֶלְבּוֹשֵׁיהּ "he proceeded to tear his clothes" IV:108, or it may
stand at the end of the sentence, as in וְקָא תָּפֵיס גַּנָּבֵי וְאָזֵל
"he proceeded to catch thieves" IV:37-38.

12.3 Rhetorical phrases II

The following rhetorical phrases occur in this section:
שְׁמַע מִנֵּהּ IV:44 lit. "he understood from it" = "he
inferred that" (#11.2). This phrase is also used as an imperative,
"conclude from that!" "draw that conclusion!" V:44
עַל אַחַת כַּמָּה וְכַמָּה IV:51 lit. "how much against one?" = "how
much the more?"
כָּל שֶׁכֵּן IV:66 lit. "all that is so" = "so much the
more," "this proves my contention"

60

12.4 Plural imperative plus suffixes

The suffixes attached to the masculine plural imperative are the
same as those attached to the 3rd masculine plural perfect (#5.12).
For example, the form אֻתְפְּסוּהִי means both 'seize him!' IV:44, and
'they seized him' IV:45.

12.5 Pael passive participle

The paradigm forms of the Pael passive participle are:

מְקַטַּל	masculine singular
מְקַטְּלָא	feminine singular
מְקַטְּלִי	masculine plural
מְקַטְּלָן	feminine plural

The forms which appear in the Corpus are:

IV:52	מְנִיחְתָּא	feminine singular
IV:105	מְחַתְּפִין	masculine plural
IV:105v.	מְחַתְּפָן	feminine plural

Note that the form מְנִיחְתָּא 'be quieted', 'be at ease' IV:52
could also be an Ithpaal participle (#9.5) מְנִיחְתָּא .

12.6 Duplication of noun

When a noun is duplicated it indicates plurality or a great amount
as, for example, in הֲווּ מַפְּקִין מִנֵּיהּ דִּיקוּלֵי דִּיקוּלֵי פְּתַרְבָּא
"they extracted from him a great deal (lit. 'baskets', 'baskets')
of fat" IV:54.

12.7 Anacoluthon

Anacoluthon invloves a break in proper grammatical sequence. A
good example is in IV:57-58, וְכִי כְּהַאי גַּוְנָא הֲוָה לֵיהּ לְרַבִּי יִשְׁמָעֵאל
בְּרַבִּי יוֹסֵי , which contextually means "a similar thing happened to
Rabbi Yishmael, son of Rabbi Yose." The problem here is that the
idiom הֲוָה לֵיהּ 'to happen to him' is separated by the preposi-
tional phrase כִּי כְּהַאי גַּוְנָא 'like this matter', which by right

should stand after it. Note also that there is a <u>casus pendens</u> (#8.8) here as well: "also for Rabbi Yishmael, son of Rabbi Yose, it happened to him" = "it happened also to Rabbi Yishmael, son of Rabbi Yose."

Chapter 13

אמר רבי יוחנן 74
אנא אישתיירי משפירי ירושלים האי מאן
76 דבעי מחזי שופריה דרבי יוחנן נייתי כסא
דכספא מבי סלקי ונמלייה פרצידיא דרומנא
78 סומקא ונהדר ליה כלילא דוורדא סומקא
לפומיה ונותביה בין שמשא לטולא ההוא
80 זהרורי מעין שופריה דר' יוחנן איני *והאמר
מר שופריה דרב כהנא מעין שופריה דרבי
82 אבהו שופריה דר' אבהו מעין שופריה דיעקב
אבינו שופריה דיעקב אבינו מעין שופריה
84 דאדם הראשון ואילו ר' יוחנלא קא חשיב ליה
שאני ר' יוחנן דהדרת פנים לא היא ליה *ר'
86 יוחנן הוה אזיל ויתיב אשערי טבילה אמר כי
סלקן בנות ישראל מטבילת מצוה לפגעו בי
88 כי היכי דלהוו להו בני שפירי כוותי גמירי
אורייתא כוותי אמרי ליה רבנן לא מסתפי מר
90 מעינא בישא אמר להו אנא *מזרעא דיוסף
קאתינא דלא שלטא ביה עינא בישא דכתיב
בן פורת יוסף בן פורת עלי עין ואמר ר' אבהו
93 אל תקרי עלי עין אלא עולי עין ר' יוסי בר חנינא
אמר מהכא וידגו לרוב בקרב הארץ מה
95 דגים שבים מים מכסים אותם ואין העין שולטת בהן אף זרעו של יוסף אין
העין שולטת בהן יומא חד הוה קא סחי ר' יוחנן בירדנא חזייה ריש לקיש
ושוור לירדנא אבתריה אמר ליה חילך לאורייתא אמר ליה שופרך לנשי א"ל אי
הדרת בך יהיבנא לך אחותי דשפירא מינאי קביל עליה בעי למיהדר לאתויי מאניה ולא מצי הדר אקרייה ואתנייה
ושוייה גברא רבא יומא חד הוו מפלגי בי מדרשא *הסייף והסכין והפגיון והרומח ומגל יד ומגל קציר מאימתי
100 מקבלין טומאה משעת גמר מלאכתן ומאימתי גמר מלאכתן אמר משיצרפם בכבשן ריש לקיש אמר
משיצחצחן במים א"ל לסטאה בלסטיותיה ידע אמר ליה ומאי אהנת לי התם רבי קרו לי הכא רבי קרו לי אמר
ליה אהנאי לך דאקרבינך תחת כנפי השכינה חלש דעתיה דרבי יוחנן חלש ריש לקיש אתאי אחתיה
קא בכיא אמרה ליה עשה בשביל בני אמר לה °עזבה יתומיך אני אחיה עשה בשביל אלמנותי אמר לה
°ואלמנותיך עלי תבטחו נח נפשיה דר' שמעון בן לקיש והוה קא מצטער ר' יוחנן בתריה טובא אמרו רבנן מאן

105ליזיל ליתביה לדעתיה ניזיל רבי אלעזר בן פדת דמחדדין שמעתתיה אזיל יתיב קמיה כל מילתא דהוה אמר
רבי יוחנן אמר ליה תניא דמסייעא לך אמר את כבר לקישא בר לקישא כי הוה אמינא מילתא הוה מקשי
לי עשרין וארבע קשייתא ומפריקנא ליה עשרין וארבעה פרוקי וממילא רווחא שמעתא ואת אמרת
תניא דמסייע לך אטו לא ידענא דשפיר קאמינא הוה קא אזיל וקרע מאניה וקא בכי ואמר היכא
109את בר לקישא היכא את בר לקישא והוה קא צוח עד דשף דעתיה [מיניה] בעו רבנן רחמי עליה ונח נפשיה

13.1 Ayin Aleph verbs

In the derived conjugations Ayin Aleph verbs become Ayin Yod.
Examples: Qal ׄ﬩ﭏׁﬢ , Pael ׄ﬩ﬢ﬩ׁ ; Qal ׄﬡﬡﬢׁ , Pael ׄﬢﬡﬢׁ . The form
ׄׄﬢﬡﬡﬢ﬩ׁ 'I have remained' IV:75 is a 1st person singular perfect
Ithpaal (#9.5) from ׄﬡﬢﬡׁ .

13.2 Double antecedent

The relative pronoun may serve as its own antecedent, e.g. ׄ﬩ﬢﬡﬢ﬩ׁ
ׄﬡﬢﬡﬢﬡׁ "he who takes bread," but the demonstrative pronoun ׄﬡﬢﬡׁ ,
or the interrogative pronoun ׄﬡﬢﬡׁ , may serve as the antecedent,
e.g. ׄ﬩ﬢﬡﬢ﬩ ﬡﬢﬡׁ or ׄ﬩ﬢﬡﬢ﬩ ﬡﬢﬡׁ . Sometimes there can be a double
antecedent with both the demonstrative and interrogative pronoun
used, as in ׄﬡﬢﬡﬢﬡ ﬡﬢﬡ ﬡﬢﬡ ﬡﬢﬡ ﬡﬢﬡ ﬡﬢﬡׁ "whoever wants
to see Rabbi Yohanan's beauty" IV:75-76. For the use of the infinitive without ׄ﬩ׁ , see #8.9.

13.3 Two objects without a preposition

Sometimes two objects will be used without a connecting preposition
between them. Examples: ׄﬡﬢﬡﬢﬡ ﬡﬢﬡﬢﬡ ﬡﬢﬡﬢﬡ ﬡﬢﬡﬢﬡ ﬡﬢﬡﬢﬡ ﬡﬢﬡﬢﬡׁ "fill it
with seeds of a red pomegranate!" IV:77-78 [for the Western plural
ׄﬡﬢﬡﬢﬡׁ , see #5.11]; ׄﬡﬢﬡﬢﬡ ﬡﬢﬡﬢﬡ ﬡﬢﬡﬢﬡ ﬡﬢﬡﬢﬡ ﬡﬢﬡﬢﬡ ﬡﬢﬡﬢﬡׁ "adorn
its brim with a crown of red roses!" IV:78-79.

13.4 The phrase ׄﬡﬢﬡﬢﬡ ﬡﬢﬡﬢﬡׁ

Because of the lack of congruence between the demonstrative ׄﬡﬢﬡׁ
'that', which is a masculine singular (#3.5), and ׄﬡﬢﬡﬢﬡׁ 'glow-
ings', 'reflexes', which is a masculine plural, the variant ׄﬡﬢﬡﬢﬡׁ

64

'those' is to be preferred in IV:79-80.

13.5 Rhetorical phrases III

The following rhetorical phrases appear in this section:

אִינְ'   IV:80 lit. "yes, it is" (< אִין הִי) = "is it really so?" "it cannot be!"

הָאֲמַר   IV:80 lit. "but he said" = "did he not say?"

מִמֵּילָא   IV:107 lit. "of itself" (< מִן אֵילָא) = "consequently"

13.6 Contraction of the demonstrative הָא

As has already been noted (#3.8), the demonstrative pronoun הָא may be used adversatively. In legal contexts it can introduce a counter argument. It may be combined with the following word, as in הָאֲמַר = הָא 'but' + אֲמַר 'he said' = "did he not say?" Other combinations with הָא include הָכְתִיב "is it not written?" and הָתָנֵי "has it not been taught?"

13.7 Verb in protasis of conditional phrase

The verb in the protasis of a conditional phrase indicating the future may be either a perfect or a participle. Thus, in the phrase אִי הֲדַרְתְּ בָּךְ "if you relent" IV:97-98, the form הֲדַרְתְּ may be either a 2nd masculine singular perfect (#7.1) הֲדַרְתְּ, or an active singular participle plus an enclitic (#11.3) הֲדַרְתְּ.

13.8 The form אִקְרַבְתָּנְ

The form אִקְרַבְתָּנְ in IV:102 is an Aphel plus a 2nd person singular suffix (cf. אֲסַנְתָּךְ #10.7). It may be analyzed as a 1st person singular imperfect, a 3rd person singular perfect, or as a 1st person plural perfect. Because the context demands a first person perfect "I have brought you near", the variant קָרֵבִתָּךְ [Pael] is to be preferred. Note that the 1st person perfect Aphel with suffix would be אוֹקְרַבְתָּךְ .

65

13.9 The term תָּנֵי

The term תָּנֵי is a passive participle form from תְּנֵי 'to teach' (#6.8), and means "it has been taught" V:32. It is a feminine because the feminine subject בָּרַיְתָא 'Baraitha' is understood. Sometimes the term תָּנֵי itself denotes the noun 'Baraitha' as, for example, in תָּנֵי דִמְסַיְּעָא לָךְ "the Baraitha supports you" IV:106. Note the use of the relative pronoun to emphasize the subject (#4.2).

14 גמ׳ *תנא היכא קאי דקתני
מאימתי ותו מאי שנא(6)דתני בערבית ברישא
16 לתני דשחרית ברישא תנא אקרא קאי
*דכתיב °בשכבך ובקומך והכי קתני זמן
קראת שמע דשכיבה אימת משעה שהכהנים
19 נכנסין לאכול בתרומתן ואי בעית אימא יליף
מברייתו של עולם דכתיב °ויהי ערב ויהי
בקר יום אחד אי הכי סיפא דקתני *ובשחר
22 מברך שתים לפניה ואחת לאחריה ובערב
מברך שתים לפניה ושתים לאחריה לתני
דערבית ברישא . תנא פתח בערבית והדר
25 תני בשחרית עד דקאי בשחרית פריש מילי
דשחרית והדר פריש מילי דערבית : אמר מר
27 משעה שהכהנים נכנסים לאכול בתרומתן.
מכדי כהנים אימת קא אכלי תרומה משעת
29 צאת הכוכבים לתני משעת צאת הכוכבים.
מלתא אגב אורחיה קמשמע לן כהנים אימת
31 קא אכלי בתרומה משעת צאת הכוכבים והא
קמשמע לן*דכפרה לא מעכבא כדתניא*ובא
השמש וטהר ביאת שמשו מעכבתו מלאכול בתרומה ואין כפרתו מעכבתו
מלאכול בתרומה.*וממאי דהאיובאהשמש ביאת השמש והאי וטהר טהר יומא
35 דילמא ביאת אורו הואומאי וטהר טהר גברא
אמר רבה בר רב שילא א״כ לימא קרא ויטהר
מאי וטהר *טהר יומא כדאמרי אינשי איערב
שמשא ואדכי יומא . במערבא הא דרבה בר
רב שילא לא שמיע להו ובעו לה מיבעיא
40 האי ובאהשמש ביאת שמשו הוא ומאיוטהר
טהר יומא או דילמא ביאת אורו הוא ומאי
וטהר טהר גברא (6) והדר פשטו לה מברייתא
מדקתני בברייתא סימן לדבר צאת הכוכבים
שמע מינה ביאת שמשו הוא ומאי וטהר טהר

67

45יומא: אמר מר משעה שהכהנים נכנסין לאכול
בתרומתן ורמינהו מאימתי קורין את שמע
בערבין משהעני נכנס לאכול פתו במלח
עד שעה שעומד ליפטר מתוך סעודתו. סיפא
ודאי פליגא אמתניתין . רישא מי לימא פליגי
אמתני'.לא עני וכהן חד שיעורא הוא. ורמינהו
51*מאימתי מתחילין לקרות ק"ש בערבית
משעה שבני אדם נכנסין לאכול פתו בערבי
שבתות דברי ר"מ וחכמים אומרים משעה
שהכהנים זכאין לאכול בתרומתן סימן לדבר
55צאת הכוכבים . ואע"פ שאין ראיה לדבר זכר
לדבר שנאמר °ואנחנו עושים במלאכה וחצים
מחזיקים ברמחים מעלות השחר עד צאת
הכוכבים ואומר °והיו לנו הלילה משמר והיום
מלאכה *מאי ואומר . וכי תימא מכי ערבא
60שמשא ליליא הוא ואינהו דמחשכי ומקדמי
ת"ש והיו לנו הלילה משמר והיום מלאכהקא
סלקא דעתך דעני ובני אדם חד שעורא הוא
ואי אמרת עני וכהן חד שעורא הוא חכמים
היינו רבי מאיר אלא שמע מינה עני שעורא
65לחוד וכהן שעורא לחוד לא עני וכהן חד
שעורא הוא ועני ובני אדם לאו חד שעורא
הוא . ועני וכהן חד שעורא הוא ורמינהו
מאימתי מתחילין לקרות שמע בערבין משעה
שקדש היום בערבי שבתות דברי ר' אליעזר
70רבי יהושע אומר משעה שהכהנים מטוהרים
לאכול בתרומתן רבי מאיר אומר משעה
שהכהנים טובלין לאכול בתרומתן אמר לו
ר' יהודה והלא כהנים מבעוד יום הם טובלים
ר' חנינא אומר משעה שעני נכנס לאכול פתו
75במלח ר' אחאי ואמרי לה ר' אחא אומר
משעה שרוב בני אדם נכנסין להסב . ואי
אמרת עני וכהן חד שעורא הוא ר' חנינאהיינו
ר' יהושע אלא לאו שמע מינה שעורא דעני
לחוד ושעורא דכהן לחוד שמע מינה . הי
80מנייהו מאוחר מסתברא דעני מאוחר דאי
אמרת דעני מוקדם ר' חנינא היינו ר' אליעזר
אלא לאו שמע מינה דעני מאוחר שמע
מינה:אמר מר אמר ליה רבי יהודה והלא
כהנים מבעוד יום הם טובלים שפיר קאמר ליהרבירבי יהודהלרבי מאירורבי מאיר
85הכי קאמר ליה מי סברת דאנא אבין השמשות דידך קא אמינא אנא אבין
השמשותדרבייוסי קאאמינא דאמר *רבי יוסי בין השמשות כהרף עין זה נכנס וזה יוצא ואי אפשר לעמוד עליו

68

14.1 Rhetorical phrases IV

The following rhetorical phrases occur in this section:

קָאֵי הֵיכָא   V:14 lit. "where does he stand?" = "on what does he base himself?"

מַאי שְׁנָא   V:15 lit. "what is different?" = "why?" "what reason is there?"

מֵאֵימָתַי   V:28 lit. "from when" = "now!" "is it not so?" [introduces an argument and often need not be translated]

אַגַּב אוֹרְחֵיהּ   V:30 lit. "by its way" = "by the way" "incidentally"

וּמְנָאַ   V:34 lit. "and from what?" = "how do you know that?" "how is it known that?"

בְּעָא אִיבָּעְיָא   V:39 lit. "they asked it to be asked" = "they asked it as a question"

וּרְמִינַן   V:46 lit. "they showed an incogruity in them" = "they pointed to a contradiction [from the following passages]"

סָלְקָא דַעְתָּךְ   V:62 lit. "your mind goes up" = "do you think?" "don't you think it?"

מִי סָבְרַתְּ   V:85 lit. "do you think?" = "you cannot think so!"

14.2 Interrogative מִי

The interrogative pronoun מִי 'who?' may introduce a general question in which case it is not translated. Examples: וּמִי מָצֵית אָמְרַתְּ סִיפָא דְּלָא כְּמַתְנִיתִין "can one assume that the first part is contrary to our Mishnah?" V:49-50 [instead of the masculine plural form סָבְרֵי the feminine singular form סָבְרָא is to be preferred, as in line 49]; מִי סָבְרַתְּ "do you think?" = "you cannot think so!" V:85.

14.3 Additional rhetorical phrases

The following are some common rhetorical phrases which do not occur
in the Corpus. A comprehensive list of such phrases may be found
in the works referred to in the Suggestions For Further Reading
on p. 131.

1. אַדְּרַבָּה (< אַדְּרַבָּה אַף) lit. "on that which is greater or
stronger" i.e. "on the contrary side is a stronger argument" =
"on the contrary"

2. אַיְּדֵי (< אַף 'דֵי דֵי) 'since' 'because', found in a phrase
like ...... תָּנֵי נַמֵי ...... אַיְּדֵי דְּתָנֵי "since he teaches...he also
teaches...."

3. אִיפְּכָא מִסְתַּבְּרָא "the reverse is the more reasonable"

4. אַלִּיבָּא (< אַף לִיבָּא) "according to"

5. מַאי נַפְקָא מִן lit. "what is the outcome from?" = "what is
the difference?" "what difference does it make?"

6. מִמַּה נַפְשָׁךְ lit. "from whatever your opinion" i.e. "from
whatever opinion you stand" = "whichever side you take" "whichever
way" "in either case"

GLOSSARY

The Glossary consists of all Hebrew and Aramaic forms which appear
in the Corpus. The forms are cited by the standard Corpus enumer-
ation, e.g. I:5; III:14, etc., see #0.4. Generally only forms
which first appear in the Corpus are listed. For example, the form
ה ‍ָ‍נ‍ ָ‍ is only listed once at I:5, since that is its first occur-
ence of many in the Corpus. The meaning given to a word in the
glossary is that which the particular word has in the context in
which it is found. Nouns are listed by their regular singular
forms. Other forms of the noun (absolute, construct, plural, with
suffixes) are listed where necessary, indented under the singular
form. For example, the absolute feminine plural form   ן ‍ ‍ֹ‍ ‍ֵ‍
'cures' will be found listed under the feminine singular regular
form א‍ָ‍ ‍ֵ‍ ‍ֹ‍‍ֵ‍. Verbs are listed by their root letters, and other
parts of the verb may be found indented according to the following
order: (1) conjugation: <u>Qal</u>, <u>Pael</u>, <u>Aphel</u>, <u>Ithpeal</u>, <u>Ithpaal</u>;
(2) tense or mood: perfect, imperfect, imperative, active parti-
ciple, passive participle, infinitive. Idioms, special phrases,
and textual comments are included at the appropriate entries.
Reference to the Manual text is indicated by the symbol #. The
following abbreviations are used in the glossary:

abbrev = abbreviated	abs = absolute	act = active
adj = adjective	adv = adverb	alt = alternate form
conj = conjunction	cons = construct	encl = enclitic
fem = feminine	Heb = Hebrew	masc = masculine
part = participle	pass = passive	plur = plural
prep = preposition	sing = singular	suff = suffix
v = variant		

Preposition joined to following word		אִ
= ﬥְ 'to' 'for' or עַﬥ 'upon' 'by',		
e.g. אִבָּאַﬡ 'at the gate' I:9, #2.12.		
'Av' a month July/August	IV:54	אָב
'father' Heb		אָב
'our father'	I:17	אָבִ׳נ׳
'father'		אִבָּא
'your father'	I:26	אִבוּךְ׳
'her father'	II:26	אִבוּהַּ׳
'your father' plur	I:28	אִבוּכוֹן
'their father'	T:45	אִבוּהוֹן
'Abbahu'	I:16	אַבָּהוּ
'city gate'	I:35	אִבוּﬥָא
'Abbaye'	I:19	אַבָּ״
'Avlat'	II:4	אַבְﬥַﬤ
'stone' Heb		אֶבֶן
plur	T:42	אַבָנִ׳ם
'Abraham'	I:6	אַבְרָהָם
'incidentally'	V:30	אַגַב + אוֹרְחִ׳ה
'meadow'	II:5	אַגְמָא
'to hire' Qal		אֲגַר
act part masc plur + 2nd encl	IV:10	אֲגִ׳ר׳תוּ
[see #11.4 for variants]		
'hire'	I:33	אַגְרָא
'wages'	II:2	
'fee'	III:70	
'while' conj	II:8	אַﬤ
'man' Heb	IV:7	אָﬤָם
'men'	V:52	בְנֵ׳ אָﬤָם
'Adam'	I:10	אָﬤָם
'so that' conj	IV:3	אַﬢ׳ﬥְﬢָא ?
'love' Heb	IV:68	אַהֲבָה

English	Ref	Hebrew
'stuffing' (feathers)	I:22v	אוּבְיָנָא
'ear'	III:68	אוּדְנָא
see אוּדְנָא	I:22	אוּבְיָנָא
'folly' Heb		אִוֶּלֶת
'his folly'	IV:69	אִוַּלְתּוֹ
'light' Heb	IV:35	אוֹר
'way'		אוֹרְחָא
'incidentally'	V:30	דֶּרֶךְ אֲגַב אוֹרְחֵיהּ
'visitor'		אוֹרְחָא
plur abs	III:84	אוֹרְחִין
'law'	IV:11	אוֹרַיְיתָא
'to go' Qal		אֲזַל
Perfect 3rd masc sing	I:29	אֲזַל
3rd fem sing	I:31	אַזְלָא
3rd masc plur	I:28	אֲזַלוּ
Imperfect 3rd masc sing	IV:105	נֵיזֵל
	IV:105	לֵיזֵל
Western form, see #9.10	T:41	יֵיזֵיל
Imperative masc sing	I:8	זֵיל
masc plur	I:27	זִילוּ
Act part masc sing	II:6	אָזֵיל
masc plur	II:5	אָזְלֵי
[for אָזֵיל as auxiliary, see #12.2]		
'Aha'	V:75	אַחָא
'Ahai'	V:75	אַחַאי
'one' Heb	V:21	אֶחָד
fem	V:22	אַחַת
'sister' Heb	IV:98	אָחוֹת
'following' adj	I:19	אַחֵר, אַחֲרִי
'one' Heb fem of אֶחָד	V:22	אַחַת
lit. "how much against one?" =		עַל אַחַת כַּמָּה וְכַמָּה
"how much the more!"	IV:51	
'sister'	IV:102	אַחָתָא
In questions expressing surprise and		אַיְ
indignation, e.g. אַיְ לֵהּ לִבֵּיהּ		

73

"do you think I don't know it myself"	IV:108	
'if' conj	I:24	אִי
'limb' here 'waist'	IV:71	אִיבָּרָא
'roof'	I:43	אִיגָּרָא
cons	III:92	אִיגַּר
'letter'	IV:36	אִיגַּרְתָּא
'he'	III:80	אִיהוּ
'there is' 'there are'	I:30	אִיכָּא
'some say'	IV:25	+ אִיכָּא דְאָמְרִי
'there was' #7.4	II:12	וַהֲוָה
'whereas' conj	IV:84	אִילּוּ
'mother' = אִימָּא	II:33	אִימָּא
'when?'	V:17	אֵימַת
'fear'	II:34	אֵימְתָא
'yes' adv	I:23	אִין
'there is/are not' Heb	II:3	אֵין
'they are not'	IV:65	אֵינָם
'is it really so?' = 'it cannot be!'	IV:80	אִינִי
'they'	III:18	אִינְהוּ
'person'	I:30	אִינָשָׁא
abs	IV:30	אִינִישׁ
'anyone' I:36		אִינִישׁ עָלְמָא
plur [I:30 אִינְשֵׁי]	II:5	אִינְשֵׁי
'indiscretion'	I:25	אִיסּוּרָא
'man' Heb	IV:67	אִישׁ
in name גּוּטָה אִישׁ טוֹב טוֹב	II:a-b	
'there is' 'there are'	I:23	אִית
= possession, #4.13		+ לִ
'woman' 'wife'	I:25	אִיתְּתָא
'that woman' = 'I' #5.3		הַהִיא אִיתְּתָא
plur	IV:97	נְשֵׁי
'to eat' 'to consume' Qal		אכל
'to traduce'	I:29	+ קוּרְצָא
Perfect 3rd masc plur	I:32	אֲכַלוּ
+ fem suff	III:92	אֲכַלוּהָ

74

Act part masc sing alt	III:91	אָכֵל
masc plur + 1st encl	II:12	אָכְלִי'ן
'to eat' Qal Heb		אֲכַל
infinitive	V:19	לְאֶכְבוֹל
'unto' Heb	IV:6	אֶל
'no' 'not' Heb	I:11	אַל
'except' 'but'	I:26	אֶלָּא
"if this were so" = 'then'	I:36	+ אֲמַצְתָה
'God'		אֱלֹהִים
'our God'	IV:40	אֱלֹהֵינוּ·
'these' Heb	IV:15	אֵלֶּה
'Elijah'	III:9	אֵלִיָּ"הוּ·
'Eliezer'	I:6	אֱלִיעֶזֶר
'to overcome' Pael		אֶלַּף
Perfect		
3rd masc sing + 3rd masc sing suff	II:36	אַלְּפֵיהּ
'widowhood' Heb	IV:103	אַלְמָנוּת
'Eleazar'	IV:22	אֶלְעָזָר
'if' Heb		אִם
'if so' abbrev אִ"כ	III:74	+ כֵּן
'why?'	I:25	אַמַּאי'
'magician'	I:18	אַמְגּוּשָׁא
'to say' Qal Heb		אָמַר
Perfect 3rd fem sing	I:10	אָמְרָה
Imperfect		
3rd masc sing + waw consecutive	III:92	וַיֹּאמַר
Act part masc sing V:58 אוֹמֵר plur	V:53	אוֹמְרִים
Niphal perfect 3rd masc sing	IV:6	נֶאֱמַר
'to say' Qal		אֲמַר
Perfect 3rd masc sing	I:21	אֲמַר
3rd fem sing	I:31	אֲמָרָה
3rd masc plur	I:23	אֲמָרוּ
Imperfect 3rd masc sing	I:34	לֵימָא
2nd masc sing	IV:2	תֵּימָא
1st sing	IV:10	אֵימָא

75

Imperative masc sing	I:8	אֱמַר
Act part masc sing	I:22	אָמַר
abbrev in אֱמ̇ד̇ן̇ = אָמַר̤פ̇ /אֱמָד̇ן̇		
masc sing + 1st encl	II:14	אָמִינָא
+ 2nd encl	V:63	אָמְרִתּ
fem sing	I:25	אָמְרָה
masc plur	I:30	אָמְרִי
'I'	I:42	אֲנָא
'we' Heb	V:56	אֲנַחְנוּ·
'I' Heb	IV:40	אֲנִי·
'cure'		אֲסוּתָא
plur abs	I:47	אָסְוָן
'Asia (Minor)'	IV:61	אַסְיָא
Niphal Heb		אֱסֹף
3rd masc plur 'they come home'	IV:6	אֱספוּן
'also'	IV:57	אַף
'just as...so'	III:55-57	אַף...אַף
'although'	IV:56	אַף עַל
'although' Heb	V:55	אַף כִּי
'even' abbrev אֹ̇פ̇	IV:52	אֲפִילוּ·
'possible' Heb	V:86	אֶפְשָׁר
'to lie in wait' Qal Heb		אָרַב
Imperfect 3rd masc sing	IV:26	אֶארֹב
'four'	III:64	אַרְבַּע
'four' [abbrev פ̇ in III:73]	III:71	אַרְבְּעָה
'lion' Heb	IV:26	אַרְיֵה
'to be tall' Pael		אָרַךְ
Act part masc sing	III:84	אַרְכִין
'widow'	III:52	אַרְמַלְתָּא
'land' Heb	IV:94	אֶרֶץ
'land'	I:23	אַרְעָא
'you'	IV:61	אַתְּ
'to come' Qal		אֲתָא
Perfect 3rd masc sing	I:19	אֲתָא
3rd fem sing	IV:102	אֲתָאת

76

Perfect 3rd masc plur	I:22	אֲתַוׄ
Imperative masc sing	IV:28	אֱקֺא
+ יֵאֱנ abbrev אָ'ׄ	V:61	
Act part masc sing	II:6	אָתֵי
+ 1st encl	IV:91	אָתֵינָאׄ
masc plur	III:63	אָתוׄ

Aphel 'to bring'

Perfect 3rd masc sing	I:20	אַ"יתֵיׄ
2nd masc sing	T:48	אַ"יתֵי'תׄ
3rd masc plur + 3rd masc		
sing suff	I:31	אַ"תֵי'ה·וׄ
	IV:37	אַ"תֵי'וּ֫ם
Imperfect 3rd masc sing	IV:76	נֵ"תֵ',
3rd masc plur	I:34	נֵ'תוׄ
Infinitive	IV:98	אַתֵו"ׄ
'you' Heb [variant has אַתֶ]	III:89	אַתֶ֫ה

ב

'in' 'at' 'by' 'amongst' prep	I:8	בֳ
Shortened form of בַר 'son of' in		
בְּרַבִּי 'son of Rabbi'	IV:37	
'where' conj	I:49	בַּאֲתַר ?
'gate'	I:7	בָּבָא
'to examine' Qal		בְּדַק
Perfect 3rd masc plur	III:12	בְּדוּקׄ
	T:46	בְּדַקוּ·
+ 3rd masc		
sing suff	T:49	בְּדַקוּם
'with' prep		בַּהֲדֵ'
'together'	II:12	+ בַּהֲדֵ'
'with me'	IV:3	בַּהֲדַאׄ
'with you'	III:3	בַּהֲדָךׄ

'to come' Qal   Heb   בוֹא

Perfect 3rd masc sing + waw consec-
utive "the sun will set"   V:32-33   וּבָא הַשֶּׁמֶשׁ

Imperfect 3rd masc sing   IV:41   יָבֹא

'to trust' Qal   Heb   בָּטַח

Imperfect 2nd masc plur   Jer. 49:11   IV:104   תִּבְטְחוּ

Hophal part masc sing   IV:52   מֻבְטָח

                                                                            בָּטַח

        'securely'   Heb   בֶּטַח

cons of בַּיִת   'בֵ

                                                                           בֵּיאוֹת

        "setting of his sun"   V:33   בֵּא שִׁמְשׁוֹ

'between'   prep   בֵּין

        'between them'   III:87   בֵּ"נ" (הם)

'evil'   IV:90   בֵּאֵשׁ

'flesh'   = בִּשְׂרָא   I:32   בֵּאֵשְׂרָא

'house'   Heb   IV:6   בַּיִת

        plur 'rooms'   I:12   בָּתִּים

'to lodge' Qal   בִּית

Perfect 3rd masc sing   T:42   בָּת

        3rd masc plur   T:47   בָּיתוּ

Infinitive   III:3   מְבִית

'house'   IV:53   בֵּיתָא

        cons   בֵּ

        'treasury'   III:14   בֵּ גִזְרָא

        'bridal chamber'   II:20-21 בֵּ גְנוֹנָא

        'banquet house'   III:87   בֵּ (וֹדֵי) קָלָא

        'king's court'   I:29   בֵּ מַלְכָּא

        'his wife' #5.1   I:24   בֵּיתֵהּ (וֹן)

'to weep' Qal   בְכָ

Act part masc sing   IV:48   בָּכֵ

        fem sing   IV:103   בָּכְיָא

'without'   prep   I:30   בְלָא

'son'   Heb   IV:38   בֵּן

        'his son' IV:49   בְּנוֹ   'my son'   IV:103   בְּנִי

78

plur cons	IV:50	בְּנֵי
'your sons'	IV:65	בְּנֵיכוֹן
'their sons'	IV:70	בְּנֵיהוֹן
'Ban'ah'	I:4	בְּנָאָה
'mattress' 'cushion'	I:24	בְּנִיתָקֵי
'to seek' 'to ask' Qal		בעי
Perfect 3rd masc sing	III:3	בְּעָא
3rd masc plur	III:b	בְּעוֹ
Imperative masc sing	II:34	בְּעִי
'to pray'	II:34-35	+ בְּעֵי רַחֲמֵי
Act part masc sing	III:88	בָּעֵי
+ lst encl	I:11	בָּעֵינָא
+ 2nd encl	IV:9	בָּעֵית
'alternatively' #11.1		אִי בָּעֵית
Pass part masc sing	I:46	בְּעִי
Ithpeal part masc plur	I:50	מִתְבַּעוֹ
fem plur	I:50v	מִתְבַּעְיָן
[or Ithpaal] fem sing = 'a question'	V:39	מִתְבַּעְיָא
'master' Heb	IV:5	בַּעַל
'to have intercourse with' Qal Heb		בָּעַל
Perfect 3rd masc plur	IV:49	בָּעֲלוּ
'morning' Heb	V:21	בֹּקֶר
'herd'	IV:63	בָּקְרָא
'son'		בְּרָא
cons = בַּ in בְּרַבַּ IV:37,#12.1	I:18	בַּר
'my son'	I:21	בְּרִי
'your son' fem sing	II:33	בְּרִיךְ
'his son'	I:29	בְּרֵיה
plur	I:25	בְּנֵי
'outside'	III:90	בָּרָא
'creation' Heb		בְּרִיָה
"creation of the world"	V:20	בְּרִיָתוֹ שֶׁל עוֹלָם
'Baraitha'	V:42	בָּרַיְתָא
'to recite a benediction' Piel Heb		בֵּרֵךְ
Act part masc sing	V:22	מְבָרֵךְ

79

'but' conj	I:39	בְּרַם
'daughter'	I:25	בְּרַתָּא
'for the sake of' Heb	IV:103	בִּשְׁבִיל
'flesh' Heb	IV:57	בָּשָׂר
see בִּשְׂרָא		בָּשְׂרָא
'daughter' Heb		בַּת
'a heavenly voice'	I:10	בַּת קוֹל
'5 qab (bottle)'	IV:72-73	+ חֲמֵשֶׁת קַבִּין
'3 qab (bottle)'	IV:73	+ תְּלָתָה קַבִּין
'9 qab (bottle)'	IV:71	+ תִּשְׁעָה קַבִּין
plur cons	IV:87	בְּנוֹת
'after' prep		בָּתַר
'after him'	IV:45	בַּתְרֵיהּ
'after her'	II:25	בַּתְרָהּ
conj	IV:45	וּבָתַר

ג

'with' 'beside' 'towards' prep	II:15	גַּבֵּי גַּב
'although' conj	IV:56	אִיגַּב עַל גַּב
'strength' Heb	IV:67	גְּבוּרָה
see גַּב	II:15	גַּבֵּי
'man'	I:24	גַּבְרָא
'great' Heb	IV:66	גָּדוֹל
'piece'	II:10	גּוּבָא
'wall'	II:23	גּוּדָא
'self'		גּוּפָא
'himself'	IV:74	גּוּפֵיהּ
'short'		גּוּצָא
abs	III:84	גּוּץ
'to cut' Qal		גֲזַז
Act part masc plur	III:84	גָּזְזֵי
'to cut' Qal		גְזַי

80

Act part masc sing alt	I:21	אֲצִיאַ
'Gehinnom' (netherworld)	IV:18	אֲגִּיהֶם
'straw'	III:11	אֲגֵּיא
'arrow'	III:11	אֲגִּיא
'wheel' 'revolution' Heb	I:13	אֲגֵּלְגֵּל
'to reveal' 'to uncover' Pael		אֲגֵּ'
Act part masc sing	I:28	אֲמֵגֵּלֵּ'
Infinitive	II:33	אֲגֵּלֵי"
Ithpeal perfect 3rd fem sing	III:91	אִיאֲגֵּלֵיאִ'
'cloak'	II:36	אֲגֵּלֵימָא
'stone'	III:80	אֲגֵּזְזֵא
'also' Heb in name לוּנֵוֹ סֵיאִ' צֵּא פֵּי	III:a-b	גֵּם
'to learn' Qal		אֲמֵר
Pass part masc plur	IV:88	אֲלֵימִי'
'to teach' Aphel		
Imperfect 1st sing + 2nd masc sing		
suff	IV:28	אַלֵימֵינָך
'finishing' Heb		אֲמֵר
cons	IV:100	אֲמֵר
'thief'	II:33	אֲגֵּזְבָא
'treasure'	III:14	אֲגֵּזְגָא
'treasury'		אֲגֵּ', אֲגֵּזְגָא
'to sleep' Qal		אֲגֵ'
Imperative	III:85	אֲגֵ'
Act part masc sing	I:8	אֲגֵיאֲ'
+ 1st encl	III:85	אֲגֵ'גָא
Aphel act part masc plur	III:83	אַמֵגֵ'
'cover' 'shadow'		אֲגֵּלֵלָא
'bridal chamber'	II:20-21	אֲגֵּלֵלָא ,אֵ'
'bone'	I:21	אֲגֵּרְמָא
'to study' Qal		גֵּרֵס
Act part masc sing	II:35	אֲגֵּרֵס
'studies'	IV:32	אֲגֵּרְסָא

81

'of' genitive indicator	I:6	דְּ
'who' relative pronoun	I:7	דְּ
'to worry' Qal		דְּאֵג
Pass part masc sing alt	II:21	דָּאֵיבָא
'his wife' #5.1	I:24	דְּבִיתְהֵי
'matter' Heb	V:43	דָּבָר
plur cons	V:53	דִּבְרֵי
'fish' Heb	IV:95	דָּג
'to multiply' Qal Heb		דָּגָה
Imperfect 3rd masc plur "may they be teeming multitudes"	IV:94	וְיִדְגּוּ לָרוֹב
'gold'	III:15	דַּהֲבָא
'honey'	III:92	דּוּבְשָׁא
See דּין		דּוּן
'to prick' 'to stick' Qal		דּוּץ
Perfect		
3rd fem sing + 3rd fem sing suff	II:23	דְּקָתַהּ
[text: דקתא , #8.3]		
'gift'	III:b	דּוֹרוֹן
'to press' Qal Heb		דָּחַק
Act part fem sing	IV:68	דּוֹחֶקֶת
Possessive suffix base		דִּיד
'mine'	III:82	דִּידִי
'yours'	V:85	דִּידָךְ
'his'	III:87	דִּידֵהּ
'ours'	T:49	דִּידַן
'image' 'figure'	I:10	דְּיוֹקָן
'inn'	III:2	דִּירָא
'innkeeper'		דִּירָא
plur	III:16	דִּירֵי
	T:43	דִּירַיָּא
'perhaps' adv	III:10	דִּלְמָא

'judge'			פָּ דָ נא
abs	I:36		פָּ דָּ ין
'to judge' <u>Qal</u>			פ'ן
Imperfect 3rd masc sing	I:35		נֶפ'וֹן
'case'	I:35		פ'ןא
abs	I:36		פ'ן
'denar' a coin	III:86		פ'ןרא
'portion' [text: ריסתנא]	II:29		פ'וסנא
'basket'	IV:54		פ'קלא
'basket'	IV:74		פ'קרא
'palm tree'	I:44		פ'קא
'beard'	I:19		פ'קןא
'inn'	T:42		פֻּ ןדֻ ק
'to be gone' <u>Ithpaal</u>			פכּ
Perfect 3rd masc sing "the day is gone"	V:38	אֶפּכּ' יוֹמָא	
'to lift up' <u>Qal</u>			פّ ל
Perfect 3rd masc sing	II:36		פَّ ל'
'blood'	I:44		פَ מא
abs	I:42		פּَ ם
'to be like' <u>Qal</u> Heb			פָּ שָּׁ ה
Act part masc sing	IV:14		פّוֹשֶׁ ה
masc plur	I:13		פّוֹשׁ 'ם
	IV:15		פّוֹשׁ 'ן
'likeness' Heb			פَ ומֻ ת
'compensation' <u>plurale tantum</u>	I:33		פּَ 'ם
'to appear' <u>Ithpeal</u>			פّ ם'
Perfect 3rd masc sing [T:45 אֶתפּَ ם']	III:9	אֶתפَّ ם'	
'mind'	IV:45		פَ עוַ ןא
'so that' conj	IV:3	פَ עוַ ןא ;	
'row'	III:61		פּَ רא
'way'	I:45		פَ רוﬞ כا
'to expound' 'to teach' <u>Qal</u>			פَ רש
Perfect 3rd masc sing	II:17	פَ רש'	

83

ה

'this' fem sing demonstrative pronoun [in T:45 expect masc הָדֵין with הָדָא]	IV:2	הָדָא
'but'	I:11	
can be joined to following word as in הָדַאֲמַר IV:80, #13.6		
'this' masc sing demonstrative pronoun	I:9	הָדֵין
'once' adv (הֲדָא + אֵיזְדָא)	II:12	הָדֵאיזְדָא
'each' 'other'		הַדָדֵי
'together'	II:12	בַּהֲדָדֵי, הֲדָדֵי
'then' adv	IV:98	הֲדֵין
'to return' Qal		הדר
Perfect 3rd masc sing	I:20	הֲדַר
used as auxiliary, #4.6		
Act part masc sing	V:24	הָדַר
+ 2nd encl [or perfect, #13.7]	IV:98	הָדַרְתְ
Infinitive	IV:98	אַהֲדָרֵי
'to crown' 'to adorn' Pael		
Imperfect 3rd masc sing	IV:78	וְהַדֵר
'to answer' Aphel		
Infinitive	IV:69	אַהֲדוּרֵי,
'glory' Heb		הֲדָרָה
'facial glory' = 'beard'	IV:85	הֲדְרַת פָּנִים
'that' masc sing demonstrative pronoun	I:18	הַהוּא
'that' fem sing demonstrative pronoun	III:49	הַהִיא
'he'	II:8	הוּא
'since' 'because' conj	I:35	הוֹאִיל וְ
See הֵוי		הֲוֵה
'to be' Qal		הוי
Perfect 3rd masc sing	I:5	הֲוָה
3rd fem sing	III:91	הֲוָת
	II:19	הֲוֵינָא
3rd masc plur	I:22	הֲווֹ
Imperfect 3rd masc sing	IV:36	לֶיהֱוֵי

84

Imperfect 3rd masc plur	IV:88	הֲווֹן
3rd fem plur	II:34	תֶּהֱוֶיַן
[expect sing תֶּהֱוֵי with variant]		
Act part masc sing [II:33 הָוֶה]	III:87	הָוֵי
'which?'	I:27	הֵי
'to be' Qal Heb		הָיָה
Perfect 3rd masc plur [V:58 וַהֲווֹ]	III:64	הָווֹ
Imperfect		
3rd masc sing + waw consecutive	V:20	וַיְהִי
Jussive 3rd masc sing	IV:12	יְהִי
'it corresponds to' 'it is this'	III:92	הַיְנוּ
'where?'	IV:9	הֵיכָא
"where does he stand?" = "on what		הֵיכָן +
does he base himself?"	V:14	
'how?'	IV:24	הֵיכִי
"what is the custom?" #11.1	IV:8	הֵיכִי דָּמֵי +
'in order that' conj	II:15-16	כִּי הֵיכִי דְּ
'feast'	III:87	הִילּוּלָא
'that' fem sing demonstrative pronoun	I:25	הַךְ
'here' adv	III:17	הָכָא
'so' 'thus' adv	I:24	הָכִי
'those' plur demonstrative pronoun	IV:79v	הָנְהוּ
'to profit' Aphel		הֲנֵי
Perfect 2nd masc sing	IV:101	אֲהֵנֵת
1st sing	IV:102	אֲהֵנִי
'those' plur demonstrative pronoun	II:5	הָנָךְ
'slaughter' Heb	IV:40	הַכִּיָּה
'decree'	IV:28	הַגְזֵרָא
		הֵילְ
"twinkling of an eye"	V:86	עֵין +
'Harpanian' from town of Harpana	IV:74	הַרְפְּנָאָה
'there'	III:6	הָתָם

ן

'and' conj	I:8	וְ
'certainly' Heb	V:49	וַדַּאי
'certainty' Heb		וַדַּאי
fem sing [expect plural וַדָּאיוֹת]	IV:51	וַדָּאוּת
'rose'	IV:78	וַרְדָּא

ז

'this' masc sing Heb	IV:14	זֶה
'reflex' 'glowing'		זָהֵר (זֹ)
plur	IV:80	זָהֵר דֹ'
'this' fem sing Heb		זוֹ
"one above the other"	I:12	זוֹ לְמַעְלָה מִזוֹ
in name זוֹ חַטְיָא בַּת זוֹ	III:a-b	
'zuz' unit of currency	III:60	זוּזָא
'bee'	III:92	זִיבּוּרָא
'forger'	III:65	זַייְפָא
'time'	T:41	זִמְנָא
'Zera'	IV:11	זֵרָא
'entitled to' Heb		זַכַּאי
plur	V:54	זַכָּאִין
'mention' Heb	V:55	זָכַר
'time' Heb	V:17	זְמַן
'to invite' Pael		זְמַן
Perfect 2nd masc sing + 1st sing suff	III:19	זְמַנְתַּן
Aphel		
Perfect 3rd masc sing + 2nd sing suff	III:89	אַזְמְנָך
1st sing + 3rd masc sing suff	III:89	אַזְמֵינְתֵּיה
Act part masc sing	III:87	מַזְמִין
'to sue'	I:37	זָיֵּנָא +

86

'cry' Heb		צְעָקָה
cons	III:92	צַעֲקַת
'gallows'	IV:48	צִקְי‍א‍| כ‍
'to impale' Qal		צְקַף
Perfect		
3rd masc plur + 3rd masc sing suff	IV:47	צְקַפוּהִי·
'to rise' (sun) Qal Heb		צְרַח
Imperfect 3rd fem sing		
"(when the sun) rises"	IV:6	תִּצְרַח
'(goatskin) bottle'	I:34	צְרוֹנִיתָ|א‍
'seed' Heb		צְרַע
'his seed'	IV:95	צַרְעוֹ
'seed'	IV:90	צִרְעָא‍|כ‍

ח

'to knock' Qal		חבֵל
Imperative masc plur	I:27	חֲבוֹלוּ·
'jug'	I:21	חָבִיתָ‍א‍|כ‍
'companion'	III:66	חַבְרָ|כ‍
Western plur #5.11	I:33	חַבְרַיָ‍א‍|כ‍
'to bind' Qal		חבַשׁ
Perfect		
3rd masc plur + 3rd masc sing suff	I:31	חַבְשׁוּהִי·|כ‍
'one'	T:41	חַדָ‍|כ‍
abs	I:19	חַד
'everyone'	III:61	כָּל חַד וְחַד
'to sharpen' Pael		חַדֵד
Pass part masc plur	IV:105	מְחַדְּדִין
[expect fem מְחַדְּדָן with variant]		
'new' Heb		חָדֵשׁ
fem	IV:8	חֲדֵשָׁה
'Eve;	I:14	חַוָּה

87

'to mock' Aphel + ל			חיך
Act part masc plur	III:7	מַחְ"כִ׳	
	T:44	מַחְ"כִי׳	
Infinitive	III:7	אַחוֹכֵ׳	
'vinegar' Heb	IV:39		חוֹמֶצֿ
"vinegar son of wine" = "wicked son		חוֹמֶצֿ בַּר	
of a righteous father"			
'to see' Qal			חז׳
Perfect			
3rd masc sing	I:35	חֲזָאk	
+ 3rd masc sing suff	IV:96	חַזְ"ה	
+ 3rd masc plur suff	T:43	חֲזַנֿוֹן	
3rd masc plur + 3rd masc plur suff	T:44	חֲזַנְנֿהֿוֹן	
Imperfect 3rd masc sing	IV:8	יֶחֱז׳	
1st plur [or 3rd masc sing]	IV:9	נֶחֱז׳	
Act part masc sing + 2nd encl	IV:30	חָזֵ׳תֿ	
Infinitive	IV:76	מֶחֱז׳	
'to hold' Hiphil Heb			חָזַק
Act part masc plur	V:57	אַחֲזִי׳קִ׳ם	
'to exhume' Qal			חלל
Act part masc sing	I:18	חָלֵלֿ	
	I:18v	חָ"לֿ	
'to preserve alive' Piel Heb			חַיָּה
Imperfect 1st sing	IV:103	אֲחַ"מֶ"ה	
'beast' Heb	IV:15		חַיָּה
"beast of the forest"	IV:13	חַ"תֿוֹ יַעַר	
'snake'	II:7		חִיוְיָא
'animal'			חֵיוְתָֿא
plur	I:23	חֵיוָתָֿא	
'to live' Qal			חי"
Act part masc sing	I:45	חָ"י	
'life' plurale tantum	I:43		חַיִּין
'strength'	IV:97		חֵילֿאֿ
'outer one' (fem) Heb	I:11		חִיצוֹנָהֿ
'wise man'	I:34		חַכִּימָהֿ

88

'to be wise' Qal		חכם
Pass part masc sing	I:35	חֲכִים
[or חֲכִים abs of חֲכִימָא]		
'sage' Heb		חָכָם
plur	V:53	חֲכָמִים
'to be weak' 'to get sick' Qal		חלש
Perfect 3rd masc sing		
"he was upset" (#7.5)	IV:102	+ חֲלַשׁ לֵיהּ
'sun' Heb	I:13	חַמָּה
'wine'	I:45	חַמְרָא
abs	I:43	חֲמַר
'donkey'	III:68	חֲמָרָא
'five' Heb	IV:73	חֲמֵשֶׁת
'bottle'	IV:71	חֵמֶת
'a nine qab bottle'	חֵמֶת בַּת תִּשְׁעָה קַבִּין	
'tavern'	IV:29	חֲנוּתָא
'Hanina'	IV:93	חֲנִינָא
'pitcher'	III:91	חַנְבָּא
'half' Heb		חֲצִי
"half of them"	V:56	חֶצְיָם
'to be impudent'		חצף
Pass part masc sing	IV:43	חָצִיף
'sword' Heb	T:46	חֶרֶב
'sword'	III:11	חַרְבָּא
'to consider' to reckon' Qal		חשב
Act part masc sing	IV:84	חָשִׁיב
'to do something at night' Pael		חשך
Act part masc plur	V:60	מַחְשְׁכֵי
+ 2nd encl	IV:3	מַחְשְׁכִיתוּ
'darkness' Heb	IV:12	חֹשֶׁךְ

'to bathe' Qal Heb			לָבַל
Act part masc plur	V:72	לֺובֵלִין	
	V:73	לֺובֵלִים	
'Mikvah' Heb	IV:86	לְבִֵלָה	
cons	IV:87	לְבֵ֫לַת	
'to be pure' 'to be clean' Qal Heb			לְהֵר
Perfect 3rd masc sing + waw consecutive			
"he/it will become pure"	V:33	וְלָהֵר	
Imperfect 3rd masc sing			
"he will be clean"	V:36	וְיַלְהַר	
Pual part masc plur	V:70	מְלֺהָרִים	
'to be clean' 'to be gone' Qal			לְהַר
Perfect 3rd masc sing			
"the day is gone"	V:34	יוֺמַא +	
"the man is clean"	V:35	גַבְרָא +	
'good' Heb			לֺוב
fem	III:b	לֺובָה	
fem plur 'fine'(stones)	T:42	לֺובוֺת	
'much' 'very' adv	II:22	לֺובָה	
"Tobe'	I:18	לֺובִי	
'shade'	IV:79	לִלֵא	
'uncleanness' Heb	IV:100	לֻמְאָה	
'bag'	II:9	לִי̣נָא	
'to add' Qal			לֺיִ
Perfect 3rd masc sing	IV:2	לֺפָא	
2nd masc sing	IV:4	לֺפַת	
1st sing	IV:2	לֺפִא	
'to be busy' Qal			לְרַד
Pass part masc plur	II:27	לְרִידִי	
'to bite' Qal			לְרַק
Act part masc sing	II:6	לַרִיק	

90

'to bring' Aphel   יבֿ

Act part masc sing + 1st encl   III:4   אוֹבֿי(לֿכֿ)

'hand' Heb   IV:50   יָ

'hand'   T:42   יָדֿא

'to know' Qal   יֿדֿע

Act part masc sing   II:35   יָדֿע

                         + 1st encl   IV:108   יָדֿע(לֿכֿ)

                   masc plur   I:22   יָדֿעֿי

Pass part masc sing   I:9   יֿדֿיֿעֿ

Infinitive   I:9   מֿיֿדֿע

'to give' Qal   יהֿבֿ

Perfect 2nd masc sing [text: יהֿבֿ ית']   II:29v   יֿהֿבֿתֿ

1st sing + 3rd masc sing suff   II:29   יֿהֿבֿתֿיֿהֿ

3rd masc plur [III:52 יֿהֿבֿו]   III:86   יֿהֿבֿו

Imperfect 3rd masc sing   III:59   אֿיֿתֿ.עֿ

Imperative masc sing   III:70   הֿבֿ

     + 3rd masc suffix   III:68   הֿבֿהֿ

     + 3rd fem suffix   III:67   יֿהֿבֿהֿ

Act part masc sing   III:71   יֿהֿבֿ

                         + 1st encl   IV:98   יֿהֿבֿיֿ(נֿא)

                   masc plur   I:33   יֿהֿבֿיֿ

'Jew'   יֿהֿוֿדֿאֿיֿ

         plur   I:30   יֿהֿוֿדֿאֿיֿ

'Judah'   III:93   יֿהֿוֿדֿהֿ

'Joshua'   IV:38   יֿהֿוֿשֿעֿ

'day'   II:11   יֿוֿמֿא

'Jose'   IV:57   יֿוֿסֿיֿ

'Joseph'   IV:12   יֿוֿסֿףֿ

'wine' Heb   IV:39   יֿיֿן

'to be able' Qal   יֿכֿלֿ

Act part masc sing + 2nd encl   IV:24   יֿכֿלֿ(תֿ)

                 masc plur   III:13   יֿכֿלֿיֿ

91

'to learn' Qal			ךֹלֽ.
Act part masc sing	V:19	ךֹ ֽלֽ֭	
'sea' Heb	IV:95		יָם
'Jacob'	I:17		יַעֲקֹב
'to go out' Qal Heb	IV:7		יְצָא
Perfect 3rd fem sing	I:10	יְצָתָה	
Imperfect 3rd masc sing	IV:7	יְצֵא	
3rd masc plur	IV:20	יְצֵאוּ.	
Infinitive construct	V:29	יְצָאת	
Act part masc sing	V:86	יְצֵאי	
Hiphil infinitive	IV:70	לְאוֹצָאָה	
'Isaac'	II:3		יִצְחָק
'exiting' Heb	IV:5		יְצִיאָה
'(evil) inclination' Heb	I:9		יֵצֶר
'(evil) inclination'	II:36		יִצְרָא
'honor'	T:47		יְקָרָא
'Jordan'	IV:96		יַרְדְּנָא
'Jerusalem'	IV:75		יְרוּשֶׁלְיִם
'Israel'	II:4		יִשְׂרָאֵל
'to sit' Qal			יְתֵב
Perfect 3rd masc sing [expect a fem]	II:23	אִיתִיבֵא	
Imperfect 3rd masc sing	I:35	לְיֵתִיב	
'to give' imperfect of יהב !	III:59	נְיֵתִיב	
Act part masc sing	II:35	יֵתִיב	
masc plur	II:4	יֵתִבֵי	
'to quiet' 'to set at rest' Pael			
Imperfect			
3rd masc sing + 3rd masc sing suffix	IV:105	לְיֵתְּבֵיהּ	
[expect 3rd fem sing suff לְיֵתְּבָהּ]			
Passive part fem sing [or Ithpaal, #12.5]	IV:52	מְיֵתְּבָא	
Aphel Imperfect			
3rd masc sing + 3rd masc sing suff	IV:79	וְנוֹתְבֵיהּ	
Act part masc plur	IV:54	מוֹתְבֵי	
'orphan' Heb	IV:103		יָתוֹם
'orphan'	III:52		יַתְמָא

כ

'like' 'as' prep	I:11	כְּ
'honor' Heb	IV:19	כָּבוֹד
'to conquer' Qal		כבש
Perfect		
3rd masc plur + 3rd masc suff (#5.12)	III:14	כְּבָשׁוּהוּ
Infinitive + masc sing suff	III:13	אֶכְבָּשׁוֹ
fem sing suff	T:46	אֶכְבָּשָׁהּ
'furnace' Heb	IV:100	כִּבְשָׁן
'priest' Heb	V:50	כֹּהֵן
plur	V:18	כֹּהֲנִים
'Kahane'	I:15	כַּהֲנָא
'fuller' Heb	III:73	כֹּבֵס
'star' Heb		כּוֹכָב
plur	V:29	כּוֹכָבִים
'all'		כּוֹלָא
cons	I:26	כָּל
'all of them'	I:28	כּוּלְהוֹן
'to such an extent' #5.7	I:35	כּוּל הַכָּא
'everyone' #5.7	II:27	כּוּל צְנַשׁ
'like' prep		כְּוָת
'like me'	IV:88	כְּוָתִי
'when' 'because' conj	I:5	כִּי
'in order that' conj	II:15-16	+ כְּדֵי, כְּ
'like' 'as' prep	IV:58	כִּי
'just as...so'	I:11	כַּ.......כֵּן
See כּוֹלָא		כָּל
'all' Heb	I:13	כָּל
'astrologer'		כַּלְדָּאִי
plur	II:20	כַּלְדָּאִי
'to destroy' Piel Heb		כִּלָּה
Imperfect 3rd masc sing	IV:41	וִיכַלֶּה
Act part masc sing	IV:40	מְכַלֶּה
'crown'	IV:78	כְּלִילָא

93

'how much?' Heb		כַּמָּה
"how much against one?" = "how much	עַל חֲדָא כַּמָּה וְכַמָּה	
the more!"	IV:51	
'thus' adv	III:90	כֵּן
'entering' Heb	IV:5	כְּנִיסָה
'to enter' Niphal Heb		כְּנַס
Act part masc sing	V:47	וְכָנֵס
masc plur	V:19	וְכָנְסִין
	V:27	וְכָנְסִים
'wing' Heb	IV:102	כָּנָף
'lap'	I:8	כַּנְפָא
'cup'	IV:30	כָּסָא
'to cover' Piel Heb		כִּסָּה
Act part masc plur	IV:95	מְכַסִּים
'to cover' Pael		כַּסִּי
Imperative masc sing	II:34	כַּסִּי
'fool' Heb	IV:69	כְּסִיל
'to be ashamed' Ithpeal		כְּסַף
Imperfect 3rd masc sing	II:16	וְיִכְסַף
Act part masc sing	II:13	מִכְסַף
'silver'	IV:77	כַּסְפָּא
'atonement'		כִּפּוּרִים
'Day of Atonement'	IV:49-50	יוֹם הַכִּפּוּרִים
'expiatory offering' Heb	V:32	כַּפָּרָה
'his expiatory offering'	V:33	כַּפָּרָתוֹ
'tribute'	III:4	כָּרְגָּא
'stomach'	IV:53	כְּרֵיסָא
'vineyard' Heb	IV:41	כֶּרֶם
'to write' Qal		כְּתַב
Perfect 3rd masc plur	I:39	כָּתְבוּ
Pass part masc sing	I:35	כְּתִיב
Infinitive	I:46	מִכְתַּב

ל

'to' 'unto' 'for' prep #2.7	I:7	לְ
'no' 'not'	I:20	לָא
'no' 'not'	I:39	לַאו
'after' Heb		לְאַחַר
'after it'	V:22	לְאַחֲרָיהָ
'brick'	III:61	לְבֵנָא
'after' conj	IV:45	לְבָתַר פ
'Laodicea' city in Asia Minor	IV:61	לוּדְקִיא
'alone' adv	V:65	לְחוֹד
'there is not' (לָ + לִית)	I:9	לֵיכָּא
'night' Heb	IV:12	לֵילָה
'night'	III:5	לֵילְיָא
'there is not'	I:26	לֵית
'why?' Heb	IV:68	לָמָה
'robber'	IV:101	לִסְטִאָה
'disrespect' Heb		לַעַז
"to cast suspicion on"	IV:70	לְהוֹצִיא ... לַעַז עַל
'profession of robber'	IV:101	לִסְטִיוּת
'according to' Heb	IV:19	לְפִי
'before' Heb	V:22	לִפְנֵי
'Lakish' in name 'Resh Lakish'	IV:4	לָקִישׁ
'Son of Lakish' = 'Resh Lakish'	IV:106	בַּר לָקִישָׁא
'before' prep		לְקַמֵי
'before him'	I:23	לְקַמֵיהּ
'tongue' Heb	IV:47	לָשׁוֹן

מ

'later' Heb	V:80	מְאוּחָר
'betrothed' Heb		מְאוֹרָס
fem	IV:49	מְאוֹרָסָה

95

'what?'	I:7	אַמַּי
'whence?'	IV:99	אֵמַּי מֵאָן
'Meir' abbrev רִ"ן 'Rabbi Meir'	V:53	אַמֵּיר
'who?' [abbrev in מַאן׳ = מֵאֵמָר פַּאן׳ 1:12]	II:15	אַמָּן
'garment'	III:90	אַמָּרְנָא
'garment' or 'weapon'	IV:98	
'ferry'	III:59	מַעֲבַּרְתָא
		עֲבַר
'handsaw'	IV:99	אֲזָי +
'scythe'	IV:99	חֲרָזֵי +
'since' conj	IV:43	אֲזֵי
'from X we learn' e.g. 'from Samuel'	II:3	
'measurement' Heb	I:11	אַמָּה
'dwelling place' Heb	IV:19	אָמוֹן
'city'	T:46	אֲמִינְתָא
'school'	IV:99	אוּלְפָנָא
'what?' used in comparative clauses	III:55	מָה
"just as...so"	III:55-57	מָה......אַף
"if X is such, then how much more is Y!"	IV:51	מָה......אַף עַל אַחַת כַּמָּה וְכַמָּה
"you might think that" #11.1	IV:2	מַמוּ דְּתֵימָא
'certain' Heb	IV:52	אוּמְחַת
'earlier' Heb	V:81	אֲקַדְּמִי
'death' Heb	II:17	מִיתָה
'death'	I:42	מִיתְנָא
'fate'(determined by astrology) Heb	II:3	מַזָּל
'region'	III:12	אַתְרָא
'to strike' Qal		מְחָ׳
Act part masc sing ##10.3, 10.4	III:65	מָחֵי
'next day'		מַחְרָא
abs	T:43	מָחָר
'to reach' Qal		מְטָא
Perfect 3rd masc sing	I:5	מְטָא
'to happen to him' #12.7	IV:57-58	לֵיהּ +
1st sing	II:14	מְטָאִי

96

'to bring' 'to offer' <u>Aphel</u> 2nd masc   III:16   אַיְתֵית

     1st sing   [T:48   אַיְתֵי]   III:17   אַיְתֵיתִי

     3rd masc plur   III:18   אַיְתִיו

          + masc plur suff   T:49   אַיְתִינְהוֹ

Act part masc plur   III:86   מַיְתֵי

'favor'   טֵיבוּתָא

     "I beg of you"   I:19   בָּעֵינָא מִטֵיבוּתָךְ

'matron'   IV:65   מַטְרוֹנִיתָא

'who?'   Heb   IV:21   מִי

Introduces general question, #14.2   V:49   מִי

'water'   I:32   מַיָּא

'question'   V:39   מִבַעֲיָא

'something'   indefinite pronoun   מִידֵי

     'any' (proof)   I:31

'word' 'matter'   II:22   מִילְּתָא

     plur   V:25   מִילֵּי

'water'   Heb   IV:95   מַ"ם

Base form for suffixes to preposition   מִן

     'from', #2.5

   IV:98   מִנְּהוֹ   I:19   מִנָּךְ

   I:38   מִנֵּיהּ   IV:44   מִנֵּהּ

   II:13   מִנָּן   I:28   מִנַּיְיכוֹ

        I:27   מִנַּיְיהוֹ

'to die'   <u>Qal</u>   מִית

Perfect 3rd masc sing   I:44   מִית

        3rd fem sing   III:85   מִיתָא

Act part masc sing   II:7   מַ"ת

        fem sing   II:21   מַיְתָא

Infinitive   I:45   מַיְמַת

'death'   Heb   II:18   מִיתָה

'brooch'   II:23   מַכְבַּנְתָּא

'from when' = "now, is it not so?"   מִכְּדֵי

     introduces an argument   V:28

'fulness'   (of a case of precious   T:42   מְלֹא

stones) = a case full of precious stones

'to fill' <u>Qal</u>   Perfect   אֱלָא

3rd masc sing + 3rd masc sing suff   III:15   אֱלָ"ה

3rd masc plur   T:44   אֱלוֹ

        + 3rd masc sing suff   T:47   אֱלוֹהי

        + 3rd masc plur suff   III:6   אֱלֻנוֹ

                                          T:43   אֱלוֹ ונוֹ

Act part masc plur   I:32   אֱלוֹ

<u>Pael</u> imperfect

3rd masc sing + 3rd masc sing suff   IV:77   נֶאַלֶ"ה

'work'   Heb   אֱלָאכָה

     'their work'   IV:100   אֱלַאכֻתַן

'experienced' Heb   III:2   אֱלוֹף

'salt'   Heb   V:47   אֱלַח

See אֱלוֹא   אֱלָ.

'king'   I:29   אֱלכָּא

'money'   אֱממָנָא

     "to exact a fine"   I:30   אַנִַּפֵ +

'consequently' see #13.5   IV:107   אֱממֵיָלָא

'from' prep with suffixes, see אֱן   I:12   אֱן

'when' 'since' conj [IV:43   אֱן]   I:45   אֱן ?

'scissors'   I:20   אֱמסֶרָא

'to hand over' <u>Qal</u>   Heb   אֱמֹסֵר

Act part masc sing   IV:39   אֱמֹוֹסֵר

'secret' Heb   IV:26   אֱמסֶֻר

'den' Heb   אֱמֹזָנֵ

     'their dens'   IV:7   אֱמֹזָנֻתֶם

'bowels' Heb   אֱמַעִים

     'my bowels'   IV:51   אֱמַ עַי

     'his bowels'   IV:50   אֱמַ עַיו

'like' prep   I:16   אֱמַעִין

'above' Heb   I:12   אֱמַעַלה

'west'   V:38   אֱמַעֱרָבָא \ אֱמַעֱרָבָא

'cave'   I:5   אֱמַעֻרָא

     plur   I:5   אֱמַעֻרָאָ

'matter' 'thing' Heb   IV:58   אֱמעֲשֶה

98

			אִלְּמָלֵי
"if this were so" 'then'		I:36	אִלְמָלֵי אֵלּוֹ
'good deed' Heb		II:16	אִמּוֹנֵי
'to be able' Qal			אָמִי
Perfect 3rd masc sing		IV:46	אָמִי
[or act part masc sing אָמִי]			
3rd masc plur		T:46	אָמוּ
[or act part masc plur אָמוּ]		T:46	
'somebody'		IV:81	אֵן
'sir' 'master'		IV:89	
'pearl' Heb			אֲסָנְדוֹרִית
plur		T:42	אֲסָנְדֵּרוֹת
'sickness'			אֲמַרְעָא
plur abs		I:46	אֲמַרְעִין
'strange' Heb			אֲסוֹרָה
'unnatural' (death)		II:18	אֲסוֹרָה
'skin'		I:32	אֲשָׁכָרא
'guard' Heb		V:58	אֲשֵׁמָר
'from' Heb		V:48	אֲמִיָּן
'to stretch' Qal			אָתַח
Act part masc plur		III:84	אָתְחִין
'when?' Heb		IV:39	אָמַי
'to compare' Qal			אָתַל
Pass part masc plur		IV:24	אֲתִלֵי
'Matnah'		I:18	אָתְנָה
'mishnah'			אָתְנִיתָא
'our Mishnah'		V:49	אָתְנִיתִין

ג

'to touch' Qal			נָגַע
Act part masc sing alt		IV:64	נָגַעה
'to drive' Heb			נָגַף
Niphal perfect 3rd masc sing		T:46	נָגַף

99

'to vow' Qal Perfect 1st sing	III:85	נָדַ֫רְתִּי	נדר
'vow'	III:85	נִדְרָ(א)	
'to be accustomed' Qal			נהג
Pass part masc plur		נְהִיגֵי	
"What is the custom?" #11.1	IV:8	מַאי נְהִיגָא	
'bread'	III:88	נַהֲמָ(א)	
'to be at ease' Qal			נוח
Perfect 3rd masc sing	IV:45	נָח	
'to die'	IV:104	+ נַ֫פְשֵׁיה	
Pass part fem sing 'pleasing'	III:15	נִיחָא	
'to place' Hiphil Heb			נוח
Perfect 3rd masc sing	IV:50	הִנִּיחַ	
'to doze' Qal			נום
Act part masc sing	IV:32	נָאֵים	
Palpel act part masc sing	IV:31	מְנַמְנֵם	
'Nahum'	III:a	נַחוּם	
'Nahman' abbrev ר"נ 'Rabbi Nahman'	II:32	נַחְמָן	
Base for suffixes to prep 'to' 'for'		נִיהֲלֵי	
	III:67	נִיהֲלָ֫ך	
	II:29	נִיהֲלֵיה	
'possessions' plurale tantum	I:26	נִכְסֵי	
'also' adv	II:3	נַמֵי	
'really'	IV:55		
'miracle' Heb			נס
plur	III:2	נִסִּים	
	T:42	נִסִּין	
'girl' Heb	IV:49	נַעֲרָה	
'to fall' Qal			נפל
Perfect 3rd masc sing	II:36	נְפַל	
Act part masc sing	I:43	נָפֵיל	
'to miscarry' Aphel			
Act part fem sing	III:66	מַפְלָא	
'to go out' 'to result' 'to owe' Qal			נפק
Perfect 3rd masc sing	I:9	נְפַק	
Act part masc sing	III:81	נָפֵיק	

Act part masc plur   III:90   צָֽבְקִ'

Aphel   perfect

3rd masc plur + 3rd masc sing suff   III:8   אַסְבְּקִוּהִי

Act part masc sing   I:30   אַמֵּיק

    fem sing   III:91   אַמְּבָקָא

    masc plur   I:38   אַמְּבְקִין'

                              IV:54   אַמְּבְקוּ'

'self' Heb   נֶֽפֶשׁ

   'himself'   IV:47   נַפְשֵׁהּ

'self'   II:15   נַֽפְשָׁא

'to save' Hiphil Heb   נָצַל

Imperfect 3rd fem sing   II:17   תֵצִּל

'different places' plurale tantum   IV:9   נִקְטִישָׁן'

'to hold' Qal   נְקַל

Act part masc sing   IV:30   נָקֵל'

'women' plur of אִיתְּתָא   IV:97   נְשֵׁ'

'to give' Qal Heb   נְתַן

Imperfect 3rd masc sing   T:46   יִתֵּן'

ס

'elder'   סָבָא

   plur   I:39   סָבִאַ'

'to dine' Hiphil   Heb   סָעַד

Infinitive   V:76   לְמִסְעַד

'to think' Qal   סְבַר

Act part masc sing + 2nd encl V:85   סָבְרַתְּ

'to be understood' Ithpaal

Part fem sing   V:80   מִסְתַּבְּרָא

'Sodom'   III:64   סְדוֹם

'witness'   סַהֲדָא

   plur   I:30   סַהֲדֵ'

'red'   IV:56   סוּמָקָא

101

'den' Heb		סֻכֹּ׃
'his den'	IV:26	סֻכֹּוֹ
'end' Heb	III:55	סֹוֹף
'to swim' Qal		סֹחֹ׳
Act part masc sing	IV:96	סָֹחֶ׳
'sword' Heb	IV:99	סֶֹיֶף
'sword'	T:45	סַֹיְיֹכֹ
'sign'	V:43	סִֹיֹאֹן
'to aid' 'to support' Pael		סֹיעֹ
Pass part masc sing	IV:108	מֹעֻ׳ץ
fem sing	IV:106	מֹעֻ׳צֹכ
'end' 'later on' 'last part'	III:88	סֹיֹפֹכ
'luggage' 'bags'	III:5	סִֹיֹפֹֹכ
'knife' Heb	IV:99	סֹכֹּיֹן
'to look' 'to see' Nithpael Heb + ג		סֹכֹל
Perfect 1st sing	I:13	נֹסֹתֹכֹֹלֹ׳
2nd masc sing	I:10	נֹסֹתֹכֹלֹתֹ
Imperfect 2nd masc sing	I:11	תֹסֹתֹכֹל
'to go up' 'to occur' Qal		סֹלֹק
Perfect 3rd masc sing	II:37	סֹלֹיֹק
Act part fem sing	III:b	סֹלֹקֹא
"do you think?" #14.1	V:62	+ סֹבֹרֹתֹ׃
fem plur	IV:87	סֹלֹקֹן
'polisher's workshop' reading with one		ב:. סֹלֹקֹן סֹלֹקֹן
of the variants סֹיֹקֹל or סֹיֹקֹלֹא	IV:77	
'drug'	IV:53	סֹמֹאֹ
'drug'		סֹמֹנֹאֹ
plur abs	I:50	סֹמֹנֹיֹן
'to dine' Qal		סֹעֹד
Infinitive	III:88	מֹסֹעֹד
'meal' Heb	V:48	סֹעֹוֹדֹֹה
'meal'	II:28	סֹעֹוֹדֹתֹאֹ
'to be afraid of' Ithpeal		סֹפֹ׳
Act part masc sing	IV:89	מֹסֹתֹפֹֹ׳

102

'doubt' Heb			סָפֵק
plur	IV:51	סְפֵיקוֹת	
'to putrify' Qal			סרח
Act part masc sing	IV:55	סָרֵיחַ	
Aphel act part masc sing	IV:56	אַסְרֵיחַ	
Act part masc plur	IV:55	סָרְחִין	
'to cling' Qal			סריך
Act part masc sing	II:25	סָרֵיךְ	
'to destroy' Qal			סתר
Perfect 3rd masc plur	T:48	סָתַרוּ	

ע

'servant' Heb	I:6		עֶבֶד
'to do' Qal			עבד
Perfect 3rd masc sing	III:90	עֲבַד	
2nd masc sing	II:11	עֲבַדְתְּ	
2nd fem sing	II:26	עֲבַדְתְּ	
Imperfect 1st sing	IV:28	אֶעֱבֵיד	
2nd masc sing	IV:29	תַּעֲבֵיד	
Act part masc sing	I:7	עָבֵיד	
masc plur	T:48	עָבְדֵי	
+ 1st encl	IV:4	עָבְדֵינָן	
'servant'	I:31		עַבְדָּא
'work' Heb			עֲבוֹדָה
'his work'	IV:7	עֲבוֹדָתוֹ	
'work'	IV:4		עֲבִידְתָּא
'to pass' Qal			עבר
Perfect 1st sing	III:74	עֲבַרִי	
2nd masc sing	III:75	עֲבַרְתְּ	
[or masc sing part + encl עָבְרַתְּ]			
Act part masc sing	III:59	עָבַר	
'to impregnate' Ithpaal			עבר

103

Imperfect 3rd masc sing

+ 3rd fem sing suff	III:67	יִצְאֻנַּהּ
'until' prep	IV:8	עַד עַ׳
'until' conj 'while' (V:25)	I:20	עַד פ
'still'		עוֹד
"while it is still"	V:73	אֲעוֹד
'world' Heb	IV:14	עוֹלָם
'to watch' 'to guard' 'to examine' Pael		עין
Perfect 3rd masc sing	I:9	עַ"יִן
Act part fem sing	I:8	מְעַ"יְנָא
'to leave' Qal Heb		עֲזַב
Imperative masc sing emphatic	IV:103	עֲזָבָה
Base for suffixes to prep 'over'		עֲלֵי
'against' 'concerning'	II:36	עֲלֵיהּ
See עַל		עֵן
'eye' Heb	IV:95	עֵין
'your eyes'	IV:49	עֵינֶיךָ
'spring' Heb	IV:92	עֵין
'eye'	II:24	עֵינָא
[expect בִּישָׁא עֵ 'evil eye']	IV:90	עֵישָׁא +
'matter' 'affair'		עִסְקָא
plur	III:93	עִסְקִין
'city' Heb	IV:8	עִיר
'to detain' 'to prevent' Pael		עכב
Act part fem sing	V:32	מְעַכְּבָא
'to be indispensable' Piel Heb		עַכֵּב
Act part fem sing + 3rd masc sing suff	V:33	מְעַכַּבְתּוֹ
'upon' 'concerning' prep II:34 עֲלָךְ		עַל
III:14 עֲלֵיהּ III:83 עֲלָהּ		
'to go up' Qal Heb		עָלָה
Act part masc plur cons	IV:93	עוֹלֵי
Infinitive construct	V:57	עֲלוֹת
'by' Heb	IV:92	עַל
'upper one' Heb	I:12	עֶלְיוֹן
'to enter' Qal		עלל

104

Imperfect 3rd masc sing	I:9	יְזִיף
Imperative masc sing	IV:29	זִיף
Act part masc sing	IV:63	צַיִף
fem sing	II:20	צַיְפָה
Pael perfect		
3rd masc sing	I:9	צַיֵּף
3rd masc plur	T:47	צַיְּפִי
+ 3rd masc sing suff	III:14	צַיְּפוּהִי
'world'	I:9	עָלְמָא
'anyone'	I:36	אֱינִשׁ עָלְמָא
'people' Heb	IV:39	עַם
'to be about to' Qal Heb		עָתַד
Act part masc sing	V:48	עָתִיד
Infinitive construct	V:86	לַעֲתוֹד
'to answer' Qal Heb		עָנָה
Imperfect 2nd masc sing apocopated	IV:69	תַּעַן
'poor man' Heb	V:47	עָנִי
'poor man'	II:27	עַנְיָא
'dust' Heb	T:46	עָפָר
'dust'	I:21	עַפְרָא
'self' Heb	I:11	עֶצֶם
'heel' Heb	I:13	עָקֵב
'Akiba' abbrev ר"ע 'Rabbi Akiba'	II:18	עֲקִיבָא
'to become dark' Qal		עֲרַב
Act part fem sing	V:59	עָרְבָא
[better אַרְבָא , cf. V:37]		
Ithpeal perfect		
3rd masc sing	V:37	אִתַּעֲרַב
'evening' Heb	IV:8	עֶרֶב
'evening' Heb	V:47	עֶרֶב
plur	V:52	עַרְבֵי
'evening' Heb	V:15	עַרְבִית
'to flee' Qal		עֲרַק
Perfect 3rd masc sing	IV:61	עֲרַק

Imperative masc sing	IV:61	צְרוֹק
'to do' Qal Heb		עֲשֵׂה
Imperative masc sing	IV:103	עֲשֵׂה
Act part masc plur	V:56	עֹשִׂים
'ten'	I:25	עֲשָׂרָה
'twenty'	IV:107	עֶשְׂרִין

פ

'dagger' Heb	IV:99	פִּגְיוֹן
'to meet' Qal		פָּגַע
Perfect 3rd masc sing	IV:42	פָּגַע
Imperfect 3rd masc plur [expect fem	IV:87	פָגְעוּ׳

יִפְגְעוּן , best is variant פֹגְעִין]

'to strike' Qal Perfect		פֵּ׳
3rd masc plur + 3rd masc sing suff	III:75	פֵּגְעוּה׳
	III:78	פֵּגְעוּה׳

In III:80 expect the sing   פֵּגְעֵה

'to strike' Qal		פֵּגַע
Act part masc sing	III:69	פֵּגַע
"Pedat'	IV:104	פֵּדָת
'mouth' Heb		פֶּה
'his mouth'	IV:46	פִּיו
'brim'	IV:79	פוּמָא
'laborer' Heb	IV:5	פּוֹעֵל
'bed'	III:83	פּוּרְיָא(תָ")
absol	III:85	פּוּרְיָא
'to leave' Niphal Heb		פָּטֵר
Infinitive	V:48	לִפְטֹר
'to be at variance' Qal		פָלֵג
Pass part fem sing	V:49	פְּלִיגָא
masc plur	V:49	פְּלִיגֵי׳

[expect fem sing פְּלִיגָא]

106

'to differ in opinion' Ithpeal			
Act part masc plur	IV:99	אִסְתַּפָּֿק	
'compared with' Heb	I:14	אֲבַֿר.	פַּֿר.
'evening'	II:26	פַּֿנְיָא
'face' Heb			פָּֿנִים
'facial glory' = 'beard'	IV:85	הַדְּרַֿת פָֿנִים
'inner one' Heb	I:12		פְּנִֿי'ם
'to disqualify' Qal perfect			פסל
3rd masc sing + 3rd masc sing suff	I:37	פַּֿסְלֵֿיהּ
'to cut off' Qal perfect			פסק
3rd masc sing + 3rd masc sing suff	II:37	פַּֿסְקֵֿיהּ
3rd masc plur	I:32	פַּֿסְקוּן·
Act part masc sing [or passive, #10.4]	III:67	פָּֿסֵיֿק
Pass part masc sing	II:10	פְּסִֿיק
'work' Heb	IV:7		פְּעַֿל
'Papa'	IV:72		פַּֿפָּֿא
'royal officer'	IV:23		פַּֿרְדַּֿכְשָׁא
'messenger'	IV:36		פַּֿרְוַֿנְקָֿא
'solution'	IV:107		פִּֿשְׁרָֿא
'seed'			פַּֿרְזְעָֿא
Western plural #5.11	IV:77	פַּֿרְזְעַֿיָּא
'to solve' Pael			פשר
Act part masc sing + 1st encl	IV:107	מְפַֿשַּׁרְנָֿא
'to redeem'			
Infinitive + 3rd masc sing suff	IV:46	פָּֿרוֹקֵֿיהּ
'to explain' Qal			פרש
Act part masc sing	V:25	פָּֿרֵֿישׁ
'to solve' Qal			פשל
Perfect 3rd masc plur	V:42	פְּשַֿׁלוּ·
Pass part fem sing 'plain' 'obvious'	IV:1	פְּשִֿׁיטָֿא
'to strip' Qal			פשל
Perfect 3rd masc plur	I:32	פְּשַֿׁלוּ·
'bread' Heb			פַּֿת
'his bread'	V:47	פַּֿתוֹ·

107

'their bread'		V:52	פִּתְהוֹן
'to open' Qal			פתח
Act part masc sing		V:24	פָּתַח

צ

'righteous' Heb		IV:19	צַדִּיק
plur		IV:17 צַדִּיקִים	
'righteous'		IV:27	צַדִּיקָא
'charity' Heb		II:17	צְדָקָה
'to cry out' Qal			צוח
Act part masc sing		IV:109 צָוַח	
See צין			צין
'scholar'		IV:31-32 אֲנַצָּן	צוֹרְבָא
'to polish' Pilpel Heb			צֶחְצַח
Imperfect 3rd masc sing + 3rd plur suff	IV:101 יְצַחְצְחֵן		
'to mark out' Pael			צין
Act part masc sing		I:5 מְצַיֵּן	
Infinitive		I:11 צַיּוּרֵי	
'to turn aside' 'to pervert' Aphel			צלף
Act part masc sing		III:65 מַצְלֵף	
'to be discreet' Qal			צנע
Pass part + 2nd encl		I:25 צְנִיעַתְּ	
'to be grieved' Ithpaal			צער
Act part masc sing		IV:104 מִצְטַעַר	
'morning'		II:24	צַפְרָא
'trouble' Heb			צָרָה
plur		IV:47 צָרוֹת	
'to be necessary' Qal			צרך
Pass part fem sing		IV:1 צְרִיכָא	
'to refine' Piel Heb			צָרַף
Imperfect			
3rd masc sing + 3rd masc plur suff		IV:100 יְצָרְפֵם	

108

ק

Use with participle, #1.11	I:5	קַאֿ
'qab' measure of capacity c. 1.16		קַֿב
quarts		
'plur'		קַֿבִּין
'a nine qab (bottle)'	IV:71	פַֿש מֶ֫שַׂע קַֿבִּין
'to receive' Piel Heb		קִֿבֵּֿל
Act part masc plur	IV:100	מְקַֿבְּֿלִין
Infinitive	IV:20	קַֿבֵּֿל
'to consent to' Pael + עַל		קַבֵּֿל
Perfect 3rd masc sing	IV:98	קַֿבִּֿיל
'grave'	I:28	קִֿבְֿרָ(ה)
'to grow' Qal		קְֿבֵֿת
Act part fem sing	III:69	קָֿבְֿתָה
'to get up early' Pael		קַֿדֵּֿם
Perfect 3rd masc sing	IV:33	קַֿדֵּֿים
Act part masc plur	V:60	מְקַֿדְּֿמִין
+ 2nd encl	IV:3	מְקַֿדְּֿמִינְהוֹן
Aphel perfect		
3rd masc sing [text קַדִּם , #11.7]	IV:32v	אַקְֿדֵּֿשׁ
Infinitive	IV:32	אַקְֿדֵּֿשׁוּתֵיהּ
'to be sanctified' Qal Heb		קָֿדֵֿשׁ
'Perfect 3rd masc sing	V:69	קָֿדֵֿשׁ
'to get up' Qal Heb		קוּם
Infinitive construct + 2nd masc suff		
"your rising"	V:17	קוּמְךָ
'to stand' Qal		קוּם
Perfect 3rd masc sing	II:8	קָֿם
3rd masc plur	III:4	קָֿמוּ
Imperative masc sing	III:85	קוּם
Act part masc sing	I:7	קָֿאֵם
+ 1st encl	II:14	קָֿאֵ֫מְנָא
masc plur	III:82	קָֿיְֿמִין

Aphel perfect

3rd masc plur + 3rd fem suff	III:92	אוֹקַהֿמָ
'monkey' Heb	I:14	קוֹף
'thorn' Heb		קוֹף
plur	IV:40	קוֹצִים
'his thorns'	IV:42	קוֹצָיו
'piece'		קוֹרֶן
"they traduced"	I:29	אכלוּ +
'difficulty'		קוּשְׁיֵא
plur	IV:107	קוּשְׁיָתָא
'to kill' Qal perfect		קטל
3rd masc sing + 3rd masc sing suff	I:44	קַטְלֵיהּ
+ 3rd masc plur suff	III:52	קַטְלִינְהוּ
3rd masc plur + 3rd masc plur suff	III:18	קַטְלִינְהוּ
Infinitive + 3rd masc sing suff	III:8	מִקְטְלֵיהּ
+ 3rd masc plur suff	T:44	מִקְטְלִינְהוּ
'cluster'	II:37	קִיבֹּרָא
'emperor'	III:b	קֵיסַר
'to happen' 'to meet' Ithpeal		קלע
Perfect 3rd masc sing [III:84 אִקְלַע]	III:73	אִיקְּלַע
Act part masc plur	IV:62	מִקַלְּעֵי
'before' prep	I:7	קַמֵּ־
'before him'	I:23	קַמֵּיהּ
See אֵמָל	IV:99	קָמִיר
'to read' Heb		קָרָא
Imperfect 2nd masc sing	IV:93	תִּקְרָ־
Act part masc plur	V:46	קוֹרִין
Infinitive	V:51	לִקְרוֹת
'to call' Qal perfect		קרא
3rd masc sing	II:27	קְרָא
+ 3rd masc sing suff	IV:43	קְרֵיהּ
3rd masc plur	IV:101	קְרוֹ
+ 3rd masc sing suff	I:34	קְרוּהוּ
Act part masc sing	IV:46	קָרֵי
masc plur	T:40	קָרוּ

110

'to teach Bible' <u>Aphel</u> perfect

3rd masc sing + 3rd masc sing suff   IV:98   אַקְרְ'ה

'to be sued' <u>Ithpeal</u>   +קֶּרִ'|

Act part masc sing   I:36   מִתְקְרֵ'

'Scripture'   IV:26   קְרָא

'midst' Heb   IV:94   קֶרֶב

'to bring near' <u>Aphel</u> perfect   קְרֵב

3rd masc sing + 2nd masc sing suff   IV:102   אַקְרִ'בְ'ךָ

    [variant <u>Pael</u> perfect קָרִ'בְ'תָּ is

      preferable, see #13.8]

'Qarha'   IV:38   קָרְחָה

'reading' Heb   קְרִ'שָׂה

      "reading of the Shema"   V:18   קְרִ'שַׂת שְׁמַע

      abbrev ק"ש in V:51

'reader'   IV:36   קָרְ'נָא

    "let the reader of the letter be   קָרְ'נָא דְּאִגַּרְתָּא אִיהוּ לֶהֱוֵי

    the messenger" = "let him who gives   פָּרְוַנְקָא

    advice carry it out"

'to split' 'to tear' <u>Qal</u>   קְרַע

Perfect 3rd masc sing   IV:108   קְרַע

       3rd masc plur   IV:53   קְרַעוּ

'stubble' Heb   T:46   קַש

'to make difficult' <u>Aphel</u>   קְשִׁ'

Act part masc sing   IV:106   מַקְשֶׁ'

'bow' Heb   T:46   קֶשֶׁת

ר

'proof' Heb   V:55   רְאָיָה

'first' Heb   I:10   רִאשׁוֹן

'head of' cons of רֵאשׁ   I:42   רֵאשׁ

    [or of Heb רֹאשׁ]

111

'Rabbi' (abbrev רׄ in I:4)	I:15		רַבִּ׳
plur |רַבָּנָן| 3וְרַבָּנָ׳ רַבָּנֵ|| in	IV:32		
'Rav'	I:16		רַב
'great' Heb			רַב
fem [Genesis 18:20]	III:93		רַבָּה
'great' adj	IV:99		רַבָּא׳
'great' adj רַבָּא׳ =	T:47		רַבָּה
'Rabba'	V:36		רַבָּה
'young girl'	III:91		רָבִ׳תָה
'to crawl' Qal Heb			רָבַב
Imperfect 3rd masc sing Ps 104:22	IV:7	יִרְבַּ3ּ׳	
'to be accustomed' Qal			רַבִל
Pass part masc sing	III:b	רְבִ׳ל	
'to flatten' (metal) 'to stretch' Pael			רדד
Perfect 3rd masc sing	IV:34	רַדֵּ׳ד	
Infinitive	IV:34	רַדּוֹדֵ׳׳	
'to run' Qal			רהט
Perfect 3rd masc sing	III:90	רְהַט	
'multitude' Heb	IV:94		רוֹב
'majority of'	V:76		
'to be enlarged' Qal			רוח
Act part fem sing	IV:107	רָוְוֹחָא׳	
'spear' Heb	IV:99		רוֹמַח
plur	V:57	רְמָחִ׳ם	
'pomegranate'	IV:77		רוּמָנָא׳
'mercy' plurale tantum			רַחֲמֵ׳א׳
'to pray'	II:35	בָּעֵ׳ +	
'young woman' Heb	III:93		רִ׳בָּה
See פִּסְיוֹנָא׳	II:29		רִ׳סְתְּנָא׳
'bread'	II:11		רִ׳פְתָּא׳
'Resh' in name "Resh Lakish"	IV:4		רֵ׳שׁ
'head' 'first part'	I:8		רֵ׳שָׁא׳
cons [possibly also Heb]	I:42	רֵישׁ	
'at first'	V:15	בְּרֵ׳שָׁא׳	

112

'worms' Heb	IV:52		רָמָה
'to cast' Aphel			רמ'
Act part masc sing + 1st encl	II:14	אָרֵמְנָא/	
[text: אָרֵמְנָא]			
masc plur + 1st encl	II:11	אָרְמֵינָן/	
'to happen' Ithpeal			
Perfect 3rd masc sing	II:23	אִתְרְמִי/	
Act part masc sing	III:85	מִתְרְמֵי/	
'to show an incongruity in' Qal perfect			רמ'
3rd masc plur + 3rd masc plur suff	V:46	רְמֵינְהוֹ	
"they showed an incongruity in them"			
= "they pointed to a contradiction"			
'to stir' Qal Heb			רָמַשׁ
Imperfect 3rd masc sing	IV:13	תִּרְמֹשׂ	
'to tend' Qal			רעי
Imperfect 3rd masc sing	III:52	לִרְעֵי	
Infinitive	III:52	מִרְעֵי	
[text: מֵרְעֵיה]			
Aphel			
Act part masc sing	III:51	מַרְעֵי	
'to be evil' Qal Heb			רָצַע
Imperfect 3rd masc sing	IV:48	יֵרַע	
'wicked'	IV:27		רַשִּׁיעָא
'wicked' Heb			רָשָׁע
plur	IV:15	רְשָׁעִים	

שׁ

'to ask' Qal			שְׁאֵיל
Imperative masc sing	IV:31	שְׁאֵיל	
'to remain' Ithpaal			שְׁאַר
Perfect 1st sing	IV:75	אִשְׁתָּאֵירִי	
'to leave' Qal perfect			שְׁבַק

113

3rd masc sing + 3rd masc sing suff	I:20	שָׁבְקֵ֫תְּה
Imperative		
masc sing + 3rd masc sing suff	I:19	שְׁבָקְ֫יהּ
Act part masc sing alt	I:28	שָׁבֵ֫קָא
+ 2nd encl	IV:27	שָׁבֵ֫קַתְּ
'to permit' Qal		שׁבק
3rd fem sing + 3rd masc sing suff	II:33	שָׁבְקֵ֫תֵהּ
'Sabbath' Heb		שַׁבָּת
plur	V:53	שַׁבָּתוֹת
'to throw' Qal		שׁדי
Perfect		
3rd masc sing + 3rd masc sing suff	II:9	שַׁדְיֵהּ
3rd masc plur	III:13	שַׁדְיוֹ
Act part masc sing	III:11	שָׁדֵי
Pass part masc sing	II:10	שְׁדֵי
'to send' Pael		שׁדר
Perfect 3rd masc plur	T:42	שַׁדַּרוּ
3rd masc plur + 3rd masc sing suff	T:47	שַׁדְּרוֹהִי
Imperfect 1st plur	III:1	נְשַׁדַּר
Infinitive	III:b	שַׁדֹּורֵי
'to make' Pael		שׁוי
Perfect		
3rd masc sing + 3rd masc sing suff	IV:99	שַׁוְיֵהּ
1st sing	II:15	שַׁוֵּיאתִ
"I pretended"		+ נַשְׁוֵיאתִ
'to smear' Qal		שׁוּף
Perfect		
3rd masc plur + fem sing suff	III:91	שָׁפוּיהַ
[expect שָׁפוּהַ]		
'to slip' Qal		שׁוּף
Perfect 3rd masc sing	IV:109	שָׁף
"he lost consciousness" #7.5		+ שַׁצֵיהּ
'beauty'	I:15	שׁוּפְרָא
'to leap' Pael		שׁור
Perfect 3rd masc sing	IV:97	שַׁוַּר

114

'wall'	III:92	שׁוּרָא
'stripe'	IV:55	שׁוּרְיָיקָא
'morning' Heb	V:21	שַׁחַר
'morning' Heb	V:16	שַׁחֲרִית
'Shela'	V:36	שֵׁלָה
'tooth'	II:37	שִׁנָּא
'sleep'	IV:53	שִׁינְתָא
'marble'	IV:53	שֵׁישָׁא
'to set' Hiphil Heb		שׁ'ת
Jussive 2nd masc sing	IV:12	תָּשֵׁת
'to lie down' Qal Heb		שָׁכַב
Infinitive cons + 2nd masc sing suff	V:17	שָׁכְבְּךָ
'to die' Qal		שכב
Act part masc sing	I:26	שָׁכִיב
'corpse'	I:18	שְׁכָבָא
'to find' Aphel		שׁכח
Perfect		
3rd masc sing	II:9	אַשְׁכַּח
+ 3rd masc sing suff	I:6	אַשְׁכְּחֵיה
3rd masc plur	III:12	אַשְׁכַּחוּ
+ 3rd masc sing suff	T:49	אַשְׁכְּחוּהַ

Ithpeal or Ithpaal   #9.5

Perfect 3rd masc sing [or אִישְׁפַּח]	III:6	וְאִישְׁתְּכַח
'lying down' Heb	V:18	שְׁכִיבָה
'divine presence' Heb	I:15	שְׁכִינָה
'to dwell' Qal Heb		שָׁכֵן
Imperfect 3rd masc sing	IV:57	יִשְׁכּוֹן
'of' Heb	IV:5	שֶׁל

IV:5 שֶׁלוֹ   IV:66 שֶׁלָנוּ   IV:51 שֶׁלְכֶם   IV:65 שֶׁלָּהֶם

'to send' Qal		שׁלח
Perfect 3rd masc sing	IV:38	שְׁלַח
'to strip' Pael		שׁלח
Imperfect 3rd masc sing	III:87	לֶשְׁלַח
[expect plur לִשְׁלְחוּ]		
Act part masc plur	III:89	מַשְׁלְחֵי

115

'to rule' Qal   Heb   (שׁלֵט)
Act part fem sing   IV:52   שַׁלֵּטֶת
'to rule' Qal   שְׁלֵט
Act part fem sing   IV:91   שַׁלְּטָא
'to complete' Hiphil   Heb   שְׁלֵם
Perfect 3rd masc sing   IV:21   הַשְׁלִים
'three'   Heb   IV:73   שְׁלֹשֶׁת
'name'   I:36   שֵׁם
'Samuel'   II:3   שְׁמוּאֵל
'heaven'   II:34   שְׁמַיָּא
'onion'   III:63   שֻׁמְכָּא
'to hear' 'to understand' Qal   שְׁמַע
Perfect 3rd masc sing   IV:44   שְׁמַע
            + 3rd masc sing suff   II:28   שַׁמְעֵיהּ
            + 3rd fem sing suff   I:24   שַׁמְעָהּ
Act part masc plur   III:89   שַׁמְעִי
Pass part masc sing   V:39   שְׁמִיעַ
Imperative masc sing   V:44   שְׁמַע
'to teach' Aphel act part masc sing   IV:3   מַשְׁמַע
     "we are taught" #11.1   + שְׁמַ
'to be heard' Ithpeal
Perfect 3rd masc sing   IV:35   אִשְׁתְּמַע
     [expect fem אִשְׁתַּמְעַת]
'Shema (prayer)'   V:18   שְׁמַע
'traditional law'   IV:107   שְׁמַעְתָא
'disquisition'   שַׁמְעַתְּתָא
     'his disquisitions'   IV:105 שְׁמַעְתָּתֵיהּ
'Simeon'   IV:22   שִׁמְעוֹן
'to guard' Qal   Heb   שְׁמַר
Act part masc sing   IV:46   שׁוֹמֵר
'sun'   Heb   IV:6   שֶׁמֶשׁ
     plur in 'twilight'   V:85   בֵּין שְׁמָשׁוֹת
'sun'   IV:54   שִׁמְשָׁא
'year'   I:19   שְׁנָה
     sing absol of   שַׁתָּא
116

'to be different' Qal		שׁנֵא
Perfect 3rd masc sing	V:15	שְׁנֵא
"What is different?" = "Why?"		מַאי שְׁנֵא
"What reason is there for this?"		
Act part masc sing	IV:85	שָׁאנֵי
'two' Heb		שְׁנַיִם
cons	I:12	שְׁנֵי
'hour'		שָׁעָא
plur	IV:29	שָׁעֵי
'time' Heb	V:18	שָׁעָה
cons "from the time"	IV:100	מִשָּׁעַת
'measure (of time)'	V:50	שָׁעוּרָא\שַׁעֲרָא
'gate' Heb		שַׁעַר
plur cons	IV:86	שַׁעֲרֵי
'good' 'beautiful' 'handsome'		שַׁפִּירָא
masc sing abs	IV:108	שַׁפִּיר
fem sing	IV:4	שַׁפִּירְתָּא
fem sing abs	IV:98	שַׁפִּירָא
masc plur	IV:75	שַׁפִּירֵי
'to cause to drink' Aphel		שׁקִי
Perfect		
3rd masc plur + 3rd masc sing suff	IV:53	אַשְׁקִיוּהִי
Act part masc plur	I:32	מַשְׁקוּ
'to take' Qal		שׁקַל
Perfect 3rd masc sing	III:70	שְׁקַל
+ 3rd masc plur suff	III:52	שַׁקְלִנְהוּ
3rd fem sing + 3rd fem sing suff	II:22	שַׁקְלָתָהּ
1st sing	III:17	שְׁקַלִי
+ 3rd masc sing suff	II:28v	שְׁקַלְתֵּיהּ
[text שַׁקְלָן]		
3rd masc plur	III:5	שְׁקַלוּ
+ 3rd masc plur suff	T:43	שַׁקְלִנְהוּ
Imperfect 3rd masc sing	III:53	נִשְׁקוּל
	III:58	לִשְׁקוּל

117

Imperative masc sing	III:14	שְׁקֹל
Act part masc sing	III:63	שָׁקֵל
+ 2nd encl	IV:27	שָׁקֵלֶת
fem sing	II:24	שָׁקְלָה
masc plur	III:61	שָׁקְלִי'
Pass part masc plur	II:15	שְׁקִילִי'
[expect 1st sing perfect שְׁקֵלִית]		
'liar'	III:65	שַׁקְּרַאי'
'awful liar'	III:65	שַׁקְּרַוְרַאי'
'to untie' <u>Qal</u> perfect		שְׁרי
3rd masc plur + 3rd masc plur suff	III:5	שְׁרַאֲרֻנְהוּ
'year' [absol I:19 שַׁתָּה]		שַׁתָּא
'to drink' <u>Qal</u>		שְׁתִי
Act part masc sing	IV:30	שָׁתֵי
'two' Heb	V:22	שְׁתַיִם

שׁ

'Sarah'	I:8	שָׂרָה
'reward' Heb		שָׂכָר
'their reward'	IV:20	שְׂכָרָן
'to rejoice' <u>Qal</u> Heb		שׂיש
Imperative masc plur	IV:50	שִׂישׂוּ'

ת

'again' adv (תּוּב)	I:44	תוּב
		תּוּן
'from' Heb	V:48	אִמְתּוּן
'decay' Heb	IV:52	תִּוְלָּה
'garlic'	III:62	תּוּמֵיא
'ox'	III:51	תּוֹרָא

118

'row'	III:61	תִּוְרָא
'under' prep	II:35	תּוֹתֵי
'beginning' Heb	III:55	תְּחִלָּה
'to begin' Hiphil Heb		תְּחַל
Act part masc plur	V:51	מַתְחִילִין
'under' prep	IV:102	תַּחַת
'lower one' Heb	I:13	תַּחְתּוֹן
'Tammuz' month June/July	IV:54	תַּאוּז
'there' adv	I:50	תַּמָּן
'eight'	III:72	תְּמָנֵי
'eight'	III:75	תַּמְנֵיא
'Tanna' lit. 'teacher'	V:14	תַּנָּא
'to teach' Qal		תְּנִי
Imperfect 3rd masc sing	V:16	תִּתְנֵי
Act part masc sing	V:14	תָּנֵי
Pass part fem sing	V:32	תַּנְיָא
Pael		
Perfect 3rd masc sing	IV:11	תַּנֵּי
'to teach Mishnah' Aphel		
Perfect 3rd masc sing		
+ 3rd masc sing suff	IV:98	אַתְנְיֵה
'to agree' Aphel		
Perfect 3rd masc plur	III:87	אַתְנֵי
'Baraitha'	IV:106	תַּנְיָא
'to seize' Qal perfect		תְּפַס
3rd masc sing + 3rd masc sing suff	I:20	תַּפְסֵיה
3rd masc plur + 3rd masc sing suff	IV:45	תַּפְסוֹהִי
Imperative		
masc sing + 3rd masc sing suff	IV:35	תַּפְסֵיה
masc plur + 3rd masc sing suff	IV:44	תַּפְסוֹהִי
Act part masc sing	IV:23	תָּפֵיס
'fat'	IV:54	תַּרְבָּא
'Terumah portion' Heb		תְּרוּמָה
'their Terumah portion'	V:19	תְּרוּמָתָן

119

'two'	III:52	שְׁתֵּי
'two'	II:10	שְׁתֵּים
'nine'	IV:71	תֵּשַׁע

INDEX

122

SUGGESTIONS FOR FURTHER READING

Since this Manual is based on the inductive method, whereby the
language is learnt directly from the Corpus of text used, it is
not meant to be comprehensive. Only that part of the morphology,
lexicon, and syntax of Babylonian Jewish Aramaic which occurs in
these texts is discussed. For the same reason full paradigms are
not given, only forms met with in the texts are illustrated in
paradigm form. Students who wish to continue their studies in
BJA grammar may be interested in the following works.

Grammars

a. for morphology

J. N. Epstein, דִּקְדּוּק אֲרָמִית בַּבְלִית (A Grammar of Babylonian
Aramaic) Jerusalem/Tel Aviv, 1960. This book should be read with
E. Y. Kutscher's important review in Leshonenu 26 (1961), 149-83.
C. Levias, A Grammar of the Aramaic Idiom Contained in the Babylonian
Talmud, Cincinnati, 1900 [Reprint: Gregg, 1971].
C. Levias, דִּקְדּוּק אֲרָמִית בַּבְלִית (A Grammar of Babylonian Aramaic),
New York, 1930 [a revised edition in Hebrew].

b. for syntax

M. L. Margolis, A Manual of the Aramaic Language of the Babylonian
Talmud, Munich, 1910.
M. Schlesinger, Satzlehre der aramäischen Sprache des babylonischen
Talmuds (Syntax of the Aramaic language of the Babylonian Talmud),
Leipzig, 1928.

Lexicons

a. _general_

M. Jastrow, _A Dictionary of the Targumim, the Talmud Babli and Yerushalmi, and the Midrashic Literature_, Philadelphia, 1903 [Reprint: Pardes, 1950].
J. Levy, _Wörterbuch über die Talmudim und Midraschim_, Berlin and Vienna, 1924.

b. _rhetorical phrases_

E. Z. Melamed, מליצות ביבליות , Jerusalem, 1947.
M. Mielziner, _Introduction to the Talmud_, New York, 1928.

Pointed editions

Students may be interested in checking the pointed editions (e.g. texts with vowels) of texts included in this Manual.
A Ehrman ed., _Babylonian and Jerusalem Talmud, El-Am edition_, Tel-Aviv, 1965 [for Berachot].
A. Steinsalz, תלמוד בבלי , Jerusalem, 1967 [for Shabbat, Sanhedrin, & Berachot].
Hatalmud Hamenuqad Hevra ltd., תלמוד בבלי מנוקד , Tel-Aviv, 1956 [for Shabbat, Baba Mezia, & Berachot].

Variants

A complete list of variants, which are occasionally referred to in the Manual by the abbreviation v., may be found in:
R. N. Rabbinovicz (Rabinovitz), _Variae Lectiones_, New York, 1867 [Reprint: New York, 1959/60].

132